CREATING A HOME

PLANNING A BETTER
KITCHEN

WARD LOCK

CONTENTS

A WARD LOCK BOOK

First published in the UK in 1997
by Ward Lock, Wellington House, 125 Strand,
London WC2R 0BB

A Cassell imprint

Copyright © Eaglemoss Publications Ltd 1997
Based on *Creating a Home*
Copyright © cover design Ward Lock 1997

Distributed in Australia
by New Holland Publishers Pty Ltd, 3/2 Aquatic Drive,
Frenchs Forest, NSW, Australia 2086

Distributed in Canada
by Cavendish Books Inc., Unit 5, 801 West 1st Street,
North Vancouver, B.C. Canada V7P 1PH

A British Library Cataloguing in Publication Data block for
this book may be obtained from the British Library

ISBN 0 7063 7661 7
Printed in Spain by Cayfosa Industria Grafica
10 9 8 7 6 5 4 3

INTRODUCTION

Creating a kitchen that looks good and works well takes more than money. You need a basic knowledge of kitchen planning, information about what equipment is on the market, and ideas.

Planning a Better Kitchen gives you all of these. It is packed with colour photographs of kitchens of every style, shape and size, backed up by drawings and scale plans showing how they can be rearranged to suit different needs. And a fully illustrated, up-to-date guide on choosing new equipment covers everything from fitted units and cookers to sinks and taps.

There is no one 'ideal' kitchen. What is perfect for you depends on your personal lifestyle, so there is a comprehensive questionnaire to fill in to help you establish your personal priorities. The first stage is planning the layout: the vital key to making your kitchen easy to work in. After setting out the ground rules for positioning kitchen units and appliances, there are five separate chapters on the typical kitchen layouts: the L-shape, the U-shape and the single line; then the big kitchen which can take an island layout, and the tiny kitchen where not a centimetre of space can be wasted.

No detail of kitchen planning is overlooked. Further chapters cover the all-important matters of storage; planning pleasant and efficient lighting; using colour to create the atmosphere you want; what materials to pick for worktops and splashbacks; even how to make use of any gaps between units.

Whether you are planning a complete refit or just wondering what sort of new cooker to buy, the fully illustrated review of kitchen units and appliances presents all the options to help you make the right decision. It covers all the latest equipment on the market: cookers of every kind, microwaves, fridges and freezers, fitted kitchen units and accessories, sinks and taps, waste disposers, cooker hoods, extractor fans and dishwashers.

Finally, there are chapters on planning and fitting out a utility room, including an illustrated guide to home laundry machines.

Planning a Better Kitchen is an essential guide to refitting or replanning your kitchen to suit today's needs.

Classic Kitchen Layouts

Surprising as it may seem, the efficient use of a kitchen depends more on how it is laid out than how big it is. Although many people long for something larger, small kitchens have plenty of potential, given the right layout.

The work sequence When you are planning the kitchen you should always aim to make the food storage, the preparation, the cooking and the serving areas as practical and energy-saving as possible.

A great deal of research has been carried out into the most efficient way to arrange a kitchen. Cooking a meal follows a predictable pattern. The three main areas of activity are food storage – fridge and food cupboards; preparation – worktops and sink; and cooking – oven and/or hob.

Although you often have to double back on yourself, expert planners have established that the most sensible layout should follow this pattern: fridge/work-top/sink/worktop/cooker and hob/work-top. If it is possible this should be arranged from left to right in an un-broken sequence.

THE WORK TRIANGLE

The sequence of storage, preparation and cooking is known as the work triangle. Obviously, the dimensions of the triangle vary, depending on the size and shape of the kitchen but the basic concept should be applied to the design of every kitchen.

Ideally, the total length of the three sides of the triangle should be between 4 and 7 metres. Distances any greater will only create needless kitchen mile-age; any less will leave you feeling cramped.

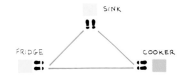

The classic layouts A kitchen can be almost any shape or size, depending on the architecture of the building. But there are just six basic layouts that, working within the guidelines of the work triangle, will give you a practical kitchen that is a pleasure to work in.

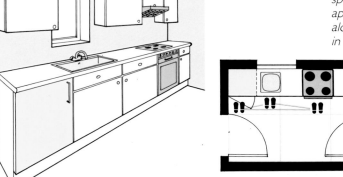

◁ *The single line*
Suitable for one or two people, this kitchen can be fitted into a very narrow space. The units and appliances are all lined up along one wall. Place the sink in the middle and choose built-under appliances so you don't lose any of the limited worktop space.

The room should be at least 2m wide to allow enough space for two people to pass each other. The single line kitchen is often a corridor and through traffic can be a problem.

Eating will have to take place elsewhere, unless a pull-out or flap-down unit can be incorporated.

scale: 1 square = 1 metre

▷ *The double galley*
Similar to the single line, the double galley has units lined along facing walls.

Most layouts will be dictated by the position of existing doors and windows but, ideally, the sink and cooker/hob should be on one side, with the fridge and storage opposite.

The double galley is a compact and easy layout for one or two people to work in, but make sure there is at least 1.2m between facing units, otherwise bending down to get something from a low-level cupboard becomes a contortionist's act. Traffic can be a problem if there is a door at either end of the room.

scale: 1 square = 1 metre

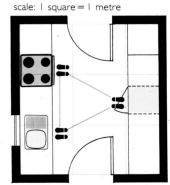

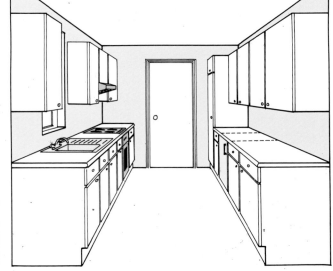

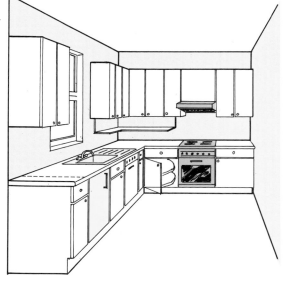

▷ The L-shape

This is a very versatile layout. The units and appliances are arranged on two adjacent walls, creating an efficient work triangle protected from through traffic.

Make sure that the corner is used to best effect – a carousel fitting inside the corner cupboard is a good solution. Separate the sink, cooker/hob and fridge with stretches of worktop to avoid the areas of activity becoming too congested.

The sides of the L can be adapted to suit an awkwardly shaped room and should be able to accommodate two cooks without them constantly getting in each other's way.

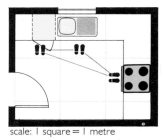

scale: 1 square = 1 metre

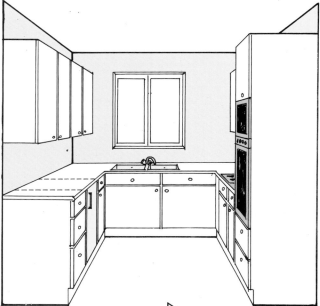

◁ The U-shape

The best kitchen layout of all, the U-shape has three walls for units and appliances, uninterrupted by through traffic – an efficient and safe arrangement in a compact area.

Scale is important: you need enough space between facing units to allow two people to work without banging into each other, while too large a space leads to unnecessary walking about. The flexible shape can often accommodate a dining area with ease.

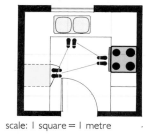

scale: 1 square = 1 metre

▷ The peninsula

In a larger room, or kitchen/dining room, the peninsula is a flexible layout. The short arm jutting out into the room divides the cooking and eating areas; it can be used to house a sink or hob with an efficient extractor hood above, or it can be a breakfast bar or serving area.

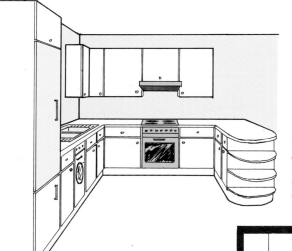

▽ The island

Essentially, the island layout is a larger version of the L- or U-shape with an additional work area in the middle. It can look stunning but is only practical in a spacious room. Careful planning is needed to avoid wasteful journeys around the island.

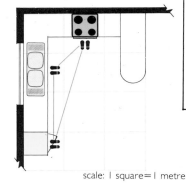

scale: 1 square = 1 metre

scale: 1 square = 1 metre

Kitchen Checkpoints

Installing a new kitchen is a major outlay and a long-term investment. Don't approach the venture in too much of a hurry as any mistakes at the planning stage will prove costly as well as a nuisance to the user.

The plan below gives you an at-a-glance guide to the main considerations in good kitchen design and over the page is a questionnaire to help organize your thoughts in detail before you start.

Keep work triangle down to minimum, usually not more than 6.6m and no shorter than 3.6m.

Task lighting provided by strip lights under wall units – there must also be adequate background lighting.

Double bowl sink – one bowl taking waste disposal. This allows for washing up and still leaves room for vegetable preparation and use of taps.

Wall and base end shelves for storage jars and cookery books.

Food storage – fridge, etc. – near to preparation area.

600mm worktop to accommodate fridges, dishwashers, etc.

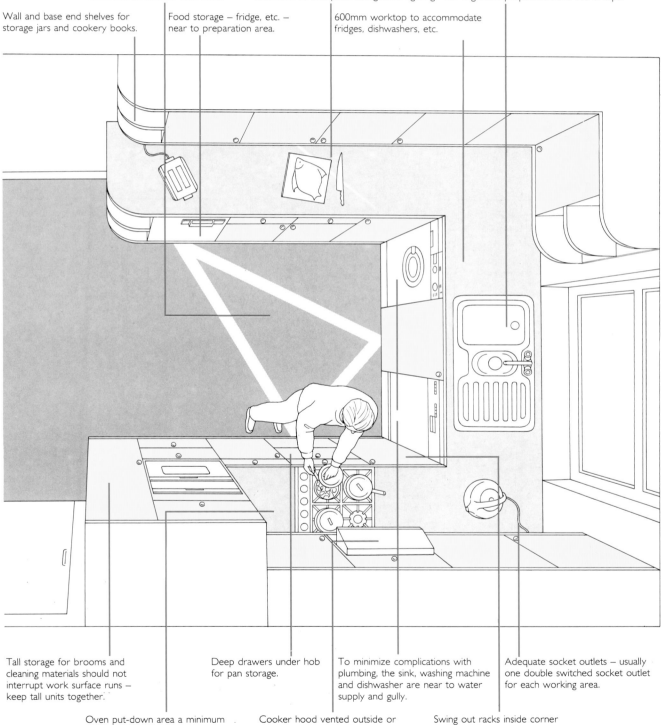

Tall storage for brooms and cleaning materials should not interrupt work surface runs – keep tall units together.

Deep drawers under hob for pan storage.

To minimize complications with plumbing, the sink, washing machine and dishwasher are near to water supply and gully.

Adequate socket outlets – usually one double switched socket outlet for each working area.

Oven put-down area a minimum width of 400mm.

Cooker hood vented outside or can be re-circulating if not on outside wall.

Swing out racks inside corner cupboard for easy access.

KITCHEN CHECKLIST

A kitchen that works and looks just the way you want it to is not easy to achieve. It requires a detailed analysis of your needs, a careful assessment of the potential of the space and a thorough investigation of the merchandise available to implement your ideas. You must also always bear in mind the basic principles of kitchen planning.

Designing a kitchen is a complicated and intricate procedure, which with our guidance you should be able to do for yourself. Professional help is now available from many retail outlets free of charge but no professional kitchen planner can help you unless you first work a bit at helping yourself. This is essential as the professional design solutions provided by planners can only be as good as your briefing.

The questionnaire below is designed to help you clarify your thoughts and to get your ideas into a workable form.

FAMILY/LIFESTYLE

☐ What do you and your family like about your present kitchen?
☐ What don't you like about the kitchen you have now?
☐ What is your idea of a dream kitchen?
☐ Who uses the kitchen and how old are they?
☐ How many people tend to use the kitchen at the same time?
　 You'll need more space if two or three people often combine to help with cooking and washing up, or if toddlers or young children are to play in the kitchen.
☐ Does anyone using the kitchen have special needs? For example, is the cook left-handed?
☐ Is anyone in the family elderly or disabled?
☐ Do you have pets that eat or sleep in the kitchen regularly?

EATING

How often and what kind of meals are taken in the kitchen and for how many people?
☐ Breakfast only.
☐ Snacks.
☐ All meals.
What kind of eating facilities are needed/preferred?
☐ A table for sit-down meals.
☐ A fold-down table.
☐ A bar with stools.
☐ A serving hatch through to the dining room.

ACTIVITIES IN THE KITCHEN

What takes place in the kitchen, apart from storing, preparing and cooking food and washing up?
☐ Eating.
☐ Laundry.
☐ Leisure activities such as watching TV, listening to music, reading, or hobbies which might involve using the sink or cooker.
☐ Homework.
☐ Entertaining.

BUDGET

☐ How much money is available to spend on your new/improved kitchen?
☐ How is finance to be provided?
　 A new kitchen is a major home improvement/investment. It should last for many years. It may be worthwhile raising extra finance (for example, by extending your mortgage or applying for a grant) to give yourself the kitchen you really want.
☐ Are you thinking of moving within the next few years?
　 If so, avoid the temptation to overspend. A new kitchen puts a certain amount of value on to a house, but usually not as much as the kitchen itself costs. The next occupants may well have very different ideas of what a kitchen should be like.

STYLE

☐ What style are you aiming to create?
☐ What colour schemes appeal?
　 Choice of colours will be influenced by the type of light your room receives as well as personal preference. Kitchens with a cold aspect tend to feel friendlier when decorated in warm colours; while those with a warmer aspect can take cooler ones. Some people find cooler colours more calming and relaxing to work with; others respond more positively to the lively nature of warm colours like red.
☐ What type of flooring do you prefer?
☐ What wall covering?

SPACE/STRUCTURE

☐ Can you work within the space available?
☐ Can you find ways of providing more space?
☐ Can you take in space from an adjacent area such as a walk-in larder, a large hall or a little-used dining room?
☐ Would removal of the wall between kitchen and living area provide an open plan arrangement to give more space for kitchen activities?
☐ Can you remove a chimney breast?
☐ Can you expand your kitchen area with an extension to your house?
☐ Could you re-site your kitchen in a larger room?
　 Always obtain professional advice before carrying out any structural alterations.
☐ Is there a boiler in the kitchen? Could it be moved, possibly to another room?
☐ How much work surface will you need, and what type do you like?
　 Consider the work surface height. This is usually dictated by the dimensions of appliances but if you are very tall or small you can adjust the height by using plinths.

APPLIANCES

☐ What kind of fuel do you plan to use?
☐ Gas.
☐ Electric.
☐ Solid fuel.
☐ A combination.
☐ What type of cooking appliances will you have?
☐ How many small electrical appliances will you have, or plan to have in the future? You will need sufficient electric sockets and storage space.
☐ What combination of fridge and freezer will you have?
☐ Do you use a lot of frozen food?
　 If you do, obviously you need a large freezer. Perhaps it would be better kept out of the kitchen, in an outhouse or garage.

SINKS

☐ What arrangement of sink(s) is best suited to your needs/space/budget?
☐ A single sink.
☐ A double sink.
☐ An extra half sink.
☐ Where do you want the draining boards?
　 Consider whether you prefer to wash up from left to right or right to left; or if you want drainers on both sides.
☐ Is the kitchen a long way from the dustbin, or do you not have room for a very large bin in the kitchen?
　 Consider installing a waste disposal.
☐ Where could you site a draining rack? If possible, attach this to the wall to save worktop space.
☐ Do you want a dishwasher, now or in the future?
　 Make sure you plan adequate space and plumbing to save additional work later.
☐ Is there enough storage space near the sink for cleaning materials, mops and buckets, tea towels, etc?

STORAGE

☐ How much food/equipment must your kitchen contain?
　 Think about all the kinds of food you have to keep in the kitchen. This will guide you towards the size of fridge/freezer needed and amount and size of cupboards/shelves required. Think about a larder.
☐ How about utensils and pots and pans?
☐ Where are you going to keep your crockery, cutlery, glasses?
　 All these considerations will determine what sort of cupboards you need. Look through manufacturers' catalogues and visit a few showrooms to see the vast choice available. Consider carousel cupboards and deep, wire drawers as well as traditional shelves and cupboards.

LIGHTING AND VENTILATION

What kind of lighting do you prefer?
☐ General overhead light.
☐ Fluorescent strips behind diffusers.
☐ Clusters or strips of spotlights.
☐ Electrified tracks.
☐ Recessed downlighters.
☐ Special under-cupboard lighting.

Is there adequate ventilation in the kitchen?
☐ Should you consider a cooker hood or an extractor fan over the cooker or hob?

LAUNDRY

☐ What kind of washing machine will there be?
☐ Will there be a tumble drier? Will it be stacked or adjacent to the machine, or a combined system to save space?
☐ Is there enough space for soap powders, pegs, laundry basket, drying rack?
☐ What facilities will you need for ironing? Where will you keep the ironing board and iron?
☐ Could the laundry be sited in the bathroom or a separate utility room?

Planning a Fitted Kitchen

Before you decide on what appliances and units to have in your kitchen, and what style you like, you need to work out exactly how everything is going to fit in, in the right place.

The first stage is to get an accurate, scaled floor plan of the room on graph paper.

Measuring for a fitted kitchen calls for more accuracy than any other room. Watch out for uneven flooring and corners that appear to be square but in fact are not 90°; care will have to be taken, especially when fitting corner cupboards or appliances.

Make a list of all the appliances you plan to have and their dimensions, not forgetting allowances for pipes, wires and ventilation at the back. Make scaled cut-outs for each appliance, and move them around on your plan, following the work triangle principles set out on pages 7-8, until you find the best possible set-up for your kitchen.

Make cut-outs of the units too, and add them to your plan. There are different sizes available; the choice varies according to the manufacturer but, usually, the more expensive the range, the more choice you will have.

Once you have finalized your plan, it's a good idea to stick masking tape down on the floor where all the cupboards and appliances are to go to check that the layout works.

If new plumbing, drainage or wiring is involved, check that your plans conform to regulations.

CUPBOARD UNITS

Wall and floor units usually come in standard widths starting at 200mm, and increasing in 100mm steps to 600mm for single cupboards and 1200mm for double units.

Wall cupboards are almost always 300mm deep and floor units are either 500mm or 600mm deep. Most appliances are 600mm deep so choose the same sized cupboard if you plan to build in the appliances. Alternatively, you could set all the floor units slightly in from the wall, using a deeper work surface to cover the gap at the back, this is ideal if you are likely to end up with lots of pipework that would be best concealed behind the units.

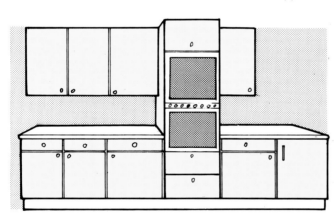

◁ *Tall units* should never be placed in the middle of a run of units as they will interrupt the work surface.

The wall space in between base units and wall cupboards can be lined with narrow shelving, about 100mm deep, or with hooks or pegs for utensils, or with a metal grid storage system.

△ *Wall units* should be positioned about 450mm above the work surface. Any lower and you won't be able to see the back of the work surface without bending down. Any higher, and the top shelves will be difficult to reach.

▷ *Corners* are the trickiest areas to deal with. It is very important that doors don't open into each other.

If you are housing an appliance near a corner you must be able to open the door to its fullest extent without banging into the wall. Here, extra tray and tea towel storage space solves the problems.

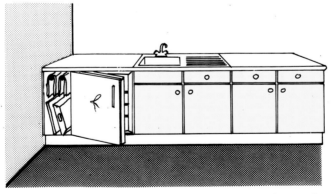

WORK SURFACES

The standard height for a work surface is 900mm. If you are tall, this may be too low, particularly for the sink, where you work with your hands below the work surface level.

It is worth experimenting to find the height that suits you, but bear in mind that units come in a standard height which will have to be built up to match unless you can alter the height by adjusting the bottom plinth. Other possibilities include setting special surfaces in the work surface at different heights, such as a butcher's block for chopping or a slab of marble for rolling out pastry.

Work surfaces are generally 600mm deep, but most manufacturers make a deeper one for peninsula units, eating areas or to cover extra-deep appliances.

APPLIANCES

Sinks, dishwashers and washing machines are usually best sited on an outside wall to allow for straightforward plumbing. Other appliances, such as ovens, hobs and fridges, should be positioned in relation to the sink, following the principles of the work triangle.

For every major appliance, allow for an electric socket below work surface level. This will avoid the need to run cables through the work surface and will free the high level sockets for smaller appliances.

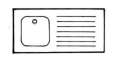

Sinks A minimum length of 1000mm for sink and draining surface is recommended. The size of sink you need will depend on how big your household is and whether or not you have a dishwasher, but the bowl should be big enough to cope with bulky items such as chopping blocks and pastry boards. Round sinks, although they can be very attractive, are usually impractical in this respect.

If there is enough space, a one-and-a-half or double bowl sink is useful, especially if one of the bowls is fitted with a waste disposal unit. Allow at least 300mm of work surface or drainer either side of the bowl for stacking dishes and pans.

Ovens Should be placed at least 300mm away from a corner to allow doors to open easily. Never position an oven within the radius of an inward-opening door. Position an eye-level oven at the end of a run of units, with plenty of work surface to one side for setting down dishes. Watch out for side-hinged doors – the handle should be on the side nearest the work surface.

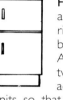

Hobs Should have at least 300mm of work surface to either side and should never be placed near windows with flapping curtains. Gas hobs should be positioned out of any draughts in case the burners blow out. Do not place a hob under wall units unless you install an extractor hood.

Dishwashers Best placed as close to the sink as possible for rinsing plates and for convenient water and waste connections. Under the draining board is often a good place for built under models. Avoid positioning a dishwasher near a corner as you will need plenty of room to open the door to its full extent for loading and unloading.

Fridges and freezers These are usually hinged on the right but some models can be hinged on either side. Allow at least 100mm between the hinge side and an adjoining wall or run of units so that you can open the door wide enough to remove shelves. For tall fridge freezers, an adjacent put-down area of around 300mm is useful.

Washing machines and tumble driers If there is no space for a separate utility room, and the washing machine/drier must be fitted in the kitchen it is more hygienic to keep them separate from the food storage and preparation zones. Position the washing machine on the same wall as the sink and/or dishwasher for ease of plumbing.

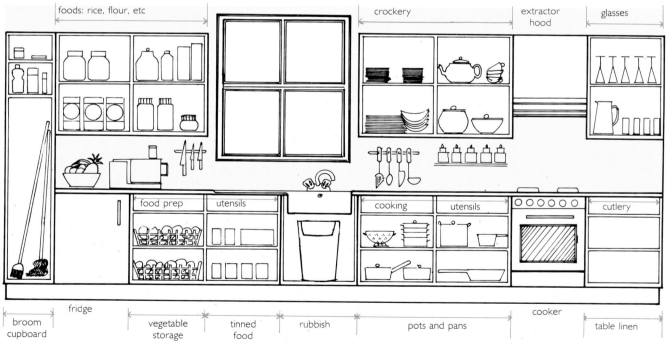

STORAGE

For greatest efficiency, organize storage around the three zones of the work triangle.

Food storage centres around the fridge, well out of the way of heat and steam. Use wall cupboards for dry goods such as flour, sugar, biscuits, etc – and store tins and jars of food in floor cupboards. Keep cleaning materials in a separate cupboard – foodstuffs tend to pick up powerful tastes and smells.

The preparation area is near the sink. Keep kitchen knives, strainers, graters, peelers and so on in drawers or hung from racks on the wall, and china and crockery handy for the washing-up and serving areas. This is also the place to keep a rubbish bin, ideally under or beside the sink.

Small appliances can be kept along the back of the work surface or in drawers or pull-out units underneath. Don't keep heavy items in wall units as they are awkward to lift down.

In the cooking area you need deep drawers or double floor cupboards for pots and pans, baking dishes and so on, and wall racks and shallow drawers for cooking utensils.

The L-shaped Kitchen

The L-shape is one of the most versatile kitchen layouts, with its units and appliances ranged along two adjacent sides. It is also one of the most functional because the work triangle isn't interrupted by through traffic.

The L layout is suitable for almost all types of room, except narrow ones or those with lots of doors, and is often used to create a kitchen in a corner of an open-plan living room or in an awkwardly shaped corner.

The L is particularly suited to kitchens that incorporate eating areas. It almost always allows space for eating – even if only a breakfast bar – and in most a table can be fitted in comfortably. Not only is it a neat, space-saving arrangement, but it is an extremely sociable set-up, allowing the cook to join in the life of the room – ideal for relaxed informal entertaining and family meals.

COOKING

The long continuous run of work surface is marvellous for cooking and, when the sides of the L are not too long, this is a very efficient and energy saving arrangement for the cook.

If one, or both, sides of the L is over-long, keep the work triangle compact and use the extra space at the long end for storage of cleaning equipment and materials and for less frequently used cooking utensils and appliances.

Once you have decided on the position of the essentials such as fridge, hob, oven and sink with its attendant plumbing, there are still plenty of ways you can vary, improve and extend the use of the L. And, of course, there are dozens of looks to choose from.

Space to work

A double sink, built-in hob unit, and fridge on the far left behind a matching door panel still leave a good stretch of continuous worktop for food preparation. There is plenty of space for two people to work at the same time in this medium-sized room and the arrangement allows space for a table for informal meals.

Utensil rack A towel rail fitted under a wall cupboard and hung with S-shaped hooks provides an attractive and handy place to keep small pots and pans and kitchen tools.

CHOICES

As well as being extremely practical, the L-shape is a very adaptable arrangement. These three kitchens, for example, are the same size with basically the same layout, but they work in different ways according to the needs and means of their owners.

There are a number of factors that will affect how you organize your kitchen once you've decided on the basic layout and where the appliances should go. You need to consider how much storage you need and where; whether to include an eating area; how many people use the room; what kind of look you want, and so on.

If you are a very keen cook and prefer buying fresh food as you need it, you won't want a lot of storage space for food, or even a very large fridge –

but you may want extra space for cooking equipment and utensils. On the other hand, you may not have the time or inclination for daily shopping, or perhaps you live in an isolated spot and tend to buy in bulk — in which case you probably want plenty of food cupboards and a large fridge and freezer.

BUDGET

Obviously, too, the amount of money available will affect your decisions. But there's no reason why you can't proceed gradually.

Once you've established the work triangle and where to put the sink, cooker and fridge, you can start with a modest set-up of cupboards set under a work surface, replacing old appliances with new, and adding extra floor and wall cupboards as you can afford them.

Cook's choice

The three L-shaped kitchens shown here illustrate the variety of uses to which the same basic layout can be put as well as the different looks that can be achieved.

The practical laminate kitchen below is designed for a keen cook who prefers

to have the maximum amount of work surface rather than an excess of cupboards. A wipeable table provides even more space for food preparation.

Floor cupboards are kept down in number with a space left under the worktop by the window for an eating or work area.

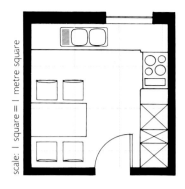

scale: 1 square = 1 metre square

Floor to ceiling

These two kitchens are designed for owners prepared to sacrifice a certain amount of worktop to gain storage space. Both rooms feature cupboards up to the ceiling but that is where the similarity ends.
▷ Open shelving and a glass-fronted cupboard contribute to the light, open look of this kitchen.
▽ A streamlined kitchen with similar features has been achieved with a totally built-in look.

SPOTLIGHT ON CORNERS

Every L-shaped kitchen turns a corner – in the best designed ones, every inch of this space is used to positive advantage.

Deep corners formed by adjacent units can be a problem but there are now dozens of well-designed corner cupboards available, and almost every manufacturer features at least one kind of carousel or lazy Susan device which fits into a floor corner unit using circular trays or shelves. And you can fit wall and floor units with bi-folding doors so it's easy to reach inside.

A simpler solution is to use open shelving around the corner, at wall or floor level, allowing everything to be seen at a glance.

The corner of the worktop is often a problem area too. It's too deep and awkward to use for work space, but it is an ideal place to keep small appliances when not in use. Another idea is to cut across the corner at an angle and build in a sink or hob, or install a built-under oven. This very smart solution allows you additional space at work surface level behind the appliance.

With all these options, there's no reason why the corner of an L-shaped kitchen should be under used.

▷ *Simple corner*
The corner worktop area is a useful place to keep wooden spoons, spices and the like next to the hob. The cupboard underneath houses a swing-out shelf unit. The angled open unit on the wall takes decorative dishes and breaks the line of solid cupboard doors.

▽ *Clever corners*
From left to right:
□ *A bi-folding door opening out on itself for an unobscured view right to the back.*
□ *A revolving carousel unit ensures nothing gets lost at the back.*
□ *A single door with two circular lazy Susan trays that swing out for easy access to small jars and spices.*
□ *A single cupboard next to a compartment for trays and wine.*

◁ **Sink solution**
A sink unit placed at an
angle across the corner.
Although this is a fairly
small kitchen, it makes
sense to sacrifice a
little cupboard space for
such a good-looking,
streamlined effect.

A wall grid between the
wall cupboard and worktop
and a hanging rail over
the sink provide
additional, attractive
storage for small
utensils.

Often a large cupboard
under the sink unit is
merely a rather scruffy area
for cleaning materials, so
the smaller cupboard space
under the sink is no
disadvantage.

The roll-up door on the
corner wall unit is
another good idea and one
less door to bang your
head on.

▷ **Slide-in option**
Cutting off the angle and
tiling the walls between top
and bottom cupboards
is the corner solution in
this cheerful kitchen.

There is a space
between the units for a
slide-in cooker (the tiles
making a sensible
splashback). This is a less
expensive alternative to a
built-in hob and built-under
oven and incidentally allows
you a double rather than a
single oven.

The space above the
cooker hood is filled with a
small wall cupboard which
aligns with the rest of the
units.

▷ **Using every spare centimetre**
This tiny room uses the L arrangement to maximum effect and usefulness. All the essentials are neatly incorporated and every bit of space is made to work for its living, with storage cupboards and shelves taken to ceiling height and a sensible amount of cupboard and drawer area. And there is just enough room for a small table – both this and the chairs fold up when not in use to give the cook more room to work.

◁ **A family kitchen**
A working kitchen which is also a pleasant place for meals with family and friends. Here the 'business' area is confined to the window recess and along one wall. Elements such as the inlaid linoleum floor and a long cloth on the round table help to define the eating areas and give it a relaxed mood.

▽ **Room to entertain**
A dining area ideal for informal entertaining is created in the opposite corner of this pastel coloured, L-shaped kitchen.

The U-shaped Kitchen

This arrangement, where units and appliances are ranged along three sides of a square or rectangle, is both functional and flexible. There is scope for choice in the positioning of worktops and appliances as well as room for plenty of storage, often on at least two complete sides of the U-shape.

Size is less of an obstacle in creating a U-shaped kitchen than awkwardly-positioned doorways. In a true U-shaped kitchen no doors break up the line of work surfaces so that the cook is not disturbed by through traffic.

FIRST CONSIDERATIONS

The U-shape lends itself to the creation of an efficient work triangle whose sides should add up to between 4 and 7 metres. Too small a work triangle could feel claustrophobic; an over-long triangle involves extra walking.

A small kitchen can accommodate a successful U-shape although it is important to allow space for two people to use the kitchen at the same time – so you need a minimum of about 1½-2 metres of space between the legs of the U-Shape.

Larger kitchens More people seem to make mistakes with large rooms than with small ones. A spacious U-shape may give plenty of work surfaces but can give rise to an elongated work triangle; it's best to confine the triangle to the base of the U-shape.

Through view
A U-shaped kitchen, with a full complement of appliances, can be fitted into the smallest of rooms, Space-saving sliding doors and an open serving hatch separate this kitchen from the interconnecting living area.

△ Room for manoeuvre

This kitchen is wide enough to allow two cooks to work together and open a drawer, cupboard, oven or fridge and stand or bend down in front of them without banging into each other.

A lot of time in the kitchen is spent at the sink – even if you do have a dishwasher. By placing the sink underneath the window, the cook has a pleasant view while working – and a sunny yellow roller blind cuts out glare on hot summer days. Teamed with matching accessories, it also brightens up dark woodwork.

USING THE SPACE

Careful siting of appliances is important for an efficient and enjoyable layout – and the three-sided U-shape gives ample room for choice.

Plan your layout carefully, using the work triangle principle to find the ideal position for your sink, hob and oven, fridge and freezer, and other appliances. Apart from considering the work triangle, remember to think about plumbing requirements, access to power, and the need to allow space for doors to open comfortably.

The continuous run of the U-shape means that there is often room for a tall larder and broom cupboard. The usual rule applies, however; position them at the end of a run to avoid interrupting the work surface.

It is usually possible to fit in an eating area, even if it is only a bar with stools tucked under it along one leg of the U-shape. If this is separated from the work area by a tall unit, the bar could be at a lower level to suit children or elderly people.

BRIGHT IDEA

Smooth rollers A pair of special rollers under a slot-in appliance makes cleaning and repairs less of a chore by allowing you to roll the machine forward. The appliance must, of course, have sufficiently long and flexible water and power connections and there needs to be about 40-50mm above it for the added height.

◁ **A narrow U-shape**
In a relatively long and narrow room such as this, it's best to confine the work area to the base of the U-shape to avoid time-wasting journeys between the sink, hob and food preparation areas.

A work surface should not normally be broken up by tall cupboards or stacked appliances. In this kitchen, the fridge/freezer and a double oven are positioned at one end of the room, near the door.

▷ **A different arrangement**
This kitchen has been rearranged so that a separate fridge and freezer have been tucked under the worktop, replacing the breakfast bar. In addition, the double oven has been replaced by a single oven slotted in directly under the hob. This has freed space for two full-height cupboards, which could act as a broom store and a larder.

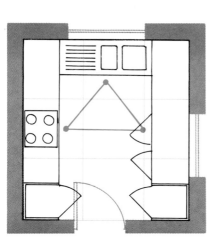

Scale: 1 square = 1 metre square

DIVIDING SPACE

A U-shaped kitchen is not necessarily self-contained. Often, the fourth wall which would close off the U-shape is absent, and instead the kitchen interconnects with another room.

Alternatively, a U-shaped kitchen can be linked to another room along one of its arms. Units can run along two walls, with the third arm making a room divider. The floor units which make up the room divider are best fitted with doors which open into both areas, with the worktop providing a convenient serving surface.

The area above the divider units can be left completely open, or open shelving or wall units can partly screen the cooking zone from a dining area. This also allows the cook to keep in touch with what is going on at the table.

▽ ▷ *Double use*
During the morning, this kitchen opens on to a breakfast area (below). Later in the day (right), the dishes are cleared away and the furniture moved aside to make room for a playpen. This practical arrangement allows a parent to prepare a meal while keeping a watchful eye on a child.

△ Breakfast bar

An extra wide worktop along one arm of the U-shape provides knee room for a breakfast bar.

◁ Extra storage

The installation of ceiling-hung units in the kitchen illustrated above greatly increases its storage capacity.

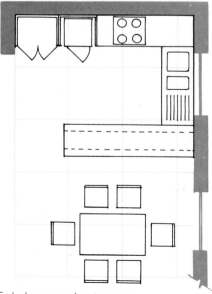

Scale: 1 square = 1 metre square

COPING WITH CORNERS

Making the best use of corners can be difficult in any kitchen and with a U-shaped layout you have two to deal with. When planning the basic layout, it is important to ensure that doors do not open into one another and that appliances are positioned at least 30 centimetres from a corner so that doors can be opened fully without banging into the wall.

Most manufacturers include corner units in their ranges – whether carousels for wall or base units or units with bi-fold doors.

▷ *A corner sink*
An unusual way of making full use of an awkward corner is to install a special sink that cuts across the corner. It's a good idea to install a strip light under the units above the sink.

▽ *Soft angles*
Corners can be used to advantage, as in this semi-circular kitchen. By angling the units and a cooker across the corners, the flow of the work surface is not interrupted. The interesting shape of the angular table adds to the visual interest and provides a useful working or breakfast table.

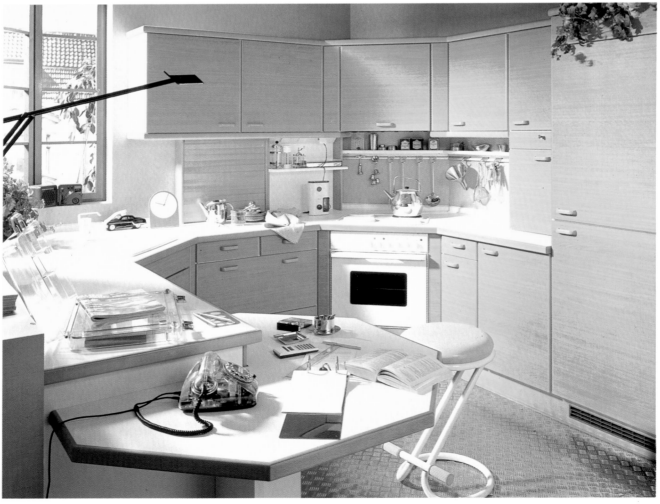

Single Line Kitchens

If your kitchen space is limited, a single line layout, where units and appliances are arranged along one wall, is often the most efficient arrangement. This layout is equally useful in a multi-purpose kitchen/dining/living room, as units and appliances can be neatly contained in one area, leaving the majority of the floor space free for dining and relaxing.

Cleverly planned, a single line kitchen can be as neat and work as well as a minute ship's galley. The road to success lies in allowing as much worktop space as possible, choosing the right units and appliances and having a flexible approach to storage.

PLANNING THE LAYOUT

The width of the room is a crucial factor in planning. You need floor space of about 1400mm so that you can move around comfortably and open doors.

Start your plan with the sink, which is best positioned in the centre of the single line, with the cooker and fridge at either end.

Ideally, there should be worktop space between the sink and appliances. If limited space means that this is impossible, place the draining side of

Perfectly plain

A single line layout is a good choice if you want to use the rest of the room for dining. Half-width doors on the wall cupboards save space when open and a laminated table such as the one shown here can double as an extra work surface if there is more than one cook.

the sink next to the cooker, so that you have somewhere to put down pans, and choose a fridge that slides under the worktop. A slide-in cooker with a pull-down glass top provides useful extra work space. Both the cooker and the fridge doors should open away from the sink for easy access. Most fridges and ovens are now sold with interchangeable hinges.

If you have a washing machine or dishwasher, tuck it underneath the draining side of the sink. This minimizes plumbing costs and means that it is quick and easy to transfer things from the sink to the machine.

Use the remaining space for base units. If possible, incorporate a larder unit with pull-out wire shelves or a carousel for storing small items. Fit an extractor in the space above the cooker between wall cupboards. If you have bought units with integral doors (special clip-ons which cover appliances), the extractor can blend into the run of cupboards. If not, look for a slimline pull-out extractor which can be positioned below a wall unit, or a standard extractor above which you can put open shelves or a cut-down cupboard.

A re-circulating charcoal filter extractor occupies less space than the ducted type where piping must be run through cupboards to the open air. If you can't afford an extractor, leave the space above the oven free, or add a couple of open shelves, starting halfway up the side of adjacent wall cupboards.

If a window interrupts the run, you could incorporate it in the overall design plan by hanging wall cupboards on either side, level with the top of the frame, then join them with a narrow overhead storage shelf. Make sure that wall cupboards allow good clearance of the work surface and check that all doors can be opened without them banging into each other.

THE CLASSIC SINGLE LINE KITCHEN

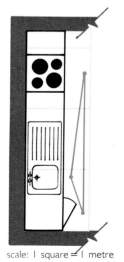

scale: 1 square = 1 metre

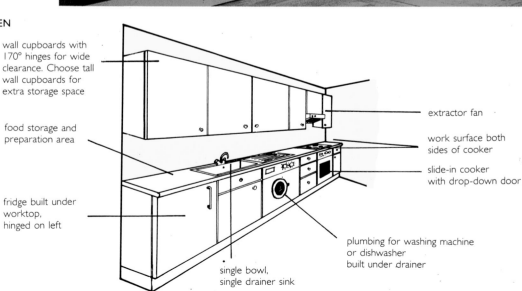

wall cupboards with 170° hinges for wide clearance. Choose tall wall cupboards for extra storage space

food storage and preparation area

fridge built under worktop, hinged on left

single bowl, single drainer sink

plumbing for washing machine or dishwasher built under drainer

extractor fan

work surface both sides of cooker

slide-in cooker with drop-down door

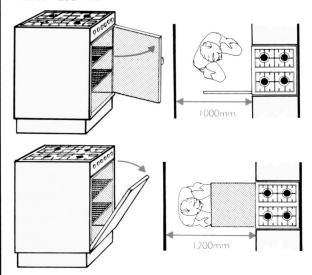

▽ Oven door clearance

Because you can stand at the side of a side-hinged oven door (below) you only need clearance of about 1000mm. You have to stand directly in front of a flap-down door (bottom), so allow slightly more room – about 1200mm.

◁ Fully integrated

This single line kitchen is part of a larger room; it has been planned to look good as well as work efficiently. The tall unit on the left houses the fridge, with two deep drawers underneath and a small cupboard above. The oven is built under the worktop with an inset hob above and an integrated pull-out extractor in the wall cupboard.

▽ Built-under bonus

Planned for maximum worktop space, there are no tall housing units in this alternative version of the same kitchen. The fridge, hinged on the left, fits under the worktop and the slide-in cooker has a toughened glass lid. A small cupboard with a work surface on top fits into the space between the cooker and end wall and is useful for putting down pans.

USING WALL SPACE

The wall facing the main run of units can also be put to good use. Narrow shelves, fitted from floor to ceiling, add invaluable extra storage space. For breakfast or light snacks, fix a hinged shelf to the wall which can be flapped up at mealtimes and folded back down against the wall to keep it out of the way when not in use. Folding chairs can lean or hang beneath the shelf when they are not needed.

CHOOSING APPLIANCES

In most single line kitchens there is not much space for appliances, so shop around for those which will work well in a limited area. Starting with the kitchen sink, there are dozens of shapes and sizes and some of the latest ranges of accessories are designed to make the most of space. Look for chopping boards and drainer baskets that fit over the sink. For a neat, streamlined look, go for an inset model in which the drainer is an integral part of the unit and choose a colour which matches the surrounding worktop.

If you have a dishwasher, you may be able to do without a draining board. Instead, fit a single inset sink with a draining rack or, if there is room, a pair of inset bowls, one with a waste disposal unit.

The new slide-in cookers are neater than the old-fashioned raised back models and are designed to match units at plinth and worktop level. A slide-in model is cheaper and takes up less space than a split-level separate oven and hob. Multi-fuel slide-ins, with a gas hob and electric oven, and models with halogen or ceramic hobs are available.

Some microwaves can be mounted between wall units and worktops – a great space saver in a single line kitchen. A microwave is a useful addition to any kitchen but it should not be seen as a replacement for a conventional oven unless it offers radiant and convected heat as well as microwaves.

▷ *Space at a premium*
As well as the usual kitchen appliances, a washing machine had to be fitted into this tiny kitchen. Tall wall cupboards stretch right up to the ceiling, making use of every inch of available space. The only practical place for the cooker was to the immediate right of the fridge (out of picture), so a slide-in model with extra insulation was chosen.

△ *Folding steps*
Maximizing storage space in a narrow kitchen often means that some shelves and cupboards are out of reach. Instead of balancing on a chair or ledge, keep some folding steps handy. These can be hung from a hook on the wall or slipped into a gap between units when folded down after use.

◁ Pull-out larder
Maximize the potential of cupboards with slide-out shelves. Here a pull-out larder unit is incorporated into a run of units under the worktop. Accessible from both sides, there is room for large bottles at the bottom, while smaller items can be kept in a shallow wire tray at the top.

With minimal cupboard space, storage must be organized efficiently. A small kitchen is no place for clutter, so store little used items in cupboards, keeping only what's absolutely essential close at hand.

▽ Breakfast bar
There is not enough room to fit any cupboards along the right hand side of this sunny yellow kitchen which has been brightened up with splashes of green.

Instead, a breakfast bar made from a narrow length of work surface to match the kitchen is attached to the wall by a hinge. This runs along the entire length so that it can be folded down against the wall when not in use.

▷ Wall-mounted boiler

Central heating boilers are no longer as large and cumbersome as they used to be. Neat, balanced flue boilers now come in a range of colours and styles, designed to fit between or be concealed inside wall cupboards.

▽ Vegetable store

The gap at the end of a run of floor units can be left open to accommodate a plastic-coated wire vegetable rack. If it is fitted with castors it can be easily pulled in and out.

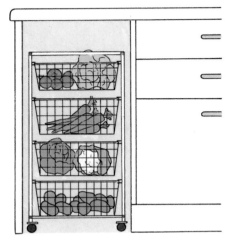

▽ Useful space

A small space between wall cupboards can be fitted with shelves, and a space between base units provides a tidy spot for trays. White walls and units with accessories picked out in a stronger colour make a kitchen feel spacious.

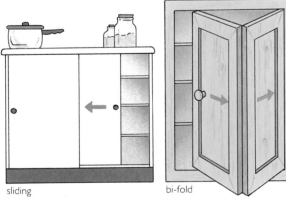

BRIGHT IDEA

sliding   bi-fold

SPACE SAVING DOORS

When it comes to kitchen doors, side-hinged are not the only choice.

Bi-fold doors, hinged in the middle, fold back on themselves to allow access to the whole cupboard.

Sliding doors take up even less room. Fixed on a pair of parallel runners, one slides alongside the other, giving access to half the cupboard at a time.

Other solutions include roller doors which slide up and over the top of the cupboard or use roller blinds to cover base units.

Island Kitchens

An island kitchen is a U or L-shaped kitchen with an additional 'bit in the middle'. Purists would argue that the island ought to be a permanent and fixed feature but in practice a table or large trolley can serve as an island.

The work triangle in an island kitchen can be very compact as the various services can be located close to each other. You can position the cooker, fridge or sink at the island although often the need to bring the necessary services (gas or electricity, and water) from the sides of the room may affect the choice.

Finding the space Island kitchens are not suitable for very small rooms. Generally they are spacious, with room all the way round the island to allow cupboard doors both on the island and on the facing run of base units to open easily. A conventional island is about 1200×1200mm square, and the minimum size is about 600×900mm. Too large an island can involve a lot of unnecessary walking, but if the kitchen isn't large enough to accommodate even a small island, it may be possible to enlarge the room, perhaps by combining the kitchen and scullery or larder.

However, an island can often be successfully fitted into a smaller room. Such islands generally serve as worktops only, with no permanent services attached. While a large room can accommodate a standard square or rectangular island, a specially designed curved or irregular-shaped island may be more suitable for a room in which space is at a premium.

In addition to the actual surface of the island, it's important to think about the areas above and below. Both can be designed to enhance the 'look' of the room as well as providing useful and accessible storage space. It is also sometimes possible to slot an appliance underneath the island worktop, and a cooker hood above an island hob is extremely useful for removing cooking smells.

A classic island

The irregularly-shaped central island in this kitchen houses both the hob and a second sink. With a large work surface, storage below and a cooker hood above, such an island can become the focal point of the kitchen.

THE ISLAND WORKTOP

The top of the island can include a hob or a sink – or it can serve purely as an extra work surface, perhaps incorporating a breakfast bar.

Connecting the services almost always means that the existing floorcovering has to be lifted so that gas, electricity and water pipes and cables can be brought to the island from the sides of the room. The connections can be run across a concrete floor before the final screed is laid, or chased into the existing screed. So long as a timber floor has sufficient depth below, services can be installed underneath.

Electricity is the simplest service to install, and allows a fridge, hob, cooker hood, and small electrical appliances to be used on the island. In contrast, if you install a sink, it needs both a supply of fresh water and an outlet to remove the waste.

A simple island can provide valuable extra working space, perhaps with special features such as an inset chopping board or marble surface for rolling out pastry.

Most islands are made to the standard height of 900mm. But if you find that this is not always ideal when you are stirring the contents of a casserole or kneading bread, for example, you can install an island at a different height.

△ *A family kitchen*
Originally, this kitchen was very small – extra space has been created by knocking two rooms into one to accommodate an island and a family breakfast bar.

The hob is located on a side wall making room on the island for a barbecue grill and a large food preparation area. The space below the worktop houses a fridge and a wine rack along with drawers and cupboards.

△ **A worktop island**
Providing an island with a gas or electricity supply can be troublesome and expensive, so it's often best to use a new island only as a worktop.

Here, the breakfast bar in the kitchen on the far left has been replaced by a more substantial dining table and the island serves both as a serving area and a working surface. The wine rack below the island is particularly useful for dinner parties.

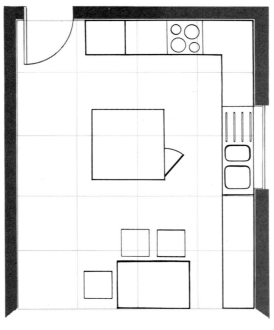

Scale: 1 square= 1 metre square

BRIGHT IDEA

A self-opening rubbish bin This ingenious rubbish bin is mounted on the inside of a cupboard door so that the lid is opened and closed by a cord when the door is opened or closed.

◁ **Country pine**
An island need not be custom-built. This pine island has been constructed from four single base units placed back to back and finished off with end panels. The worktop includes a gas hob and an electric deep fryer and hotplate.

▽ **A movable island**
The trolley in this kitchen makes a movable island, and it is ideal for small as well as more spacious kitchens. The solid maple chopping surface should give years of service, and the vegetable basket, drawer and storage shelf provide a useful place to keep fresh foods and implements. Mounted on four locking castors, the trolley can be moved out of the way when not required.

Planning a Tiny Kitchen

Nowhere is planning more critical than when designing a tiny – as opposed to a restricted or small – kitchen. Squeezing in enough working and storage space can pose a real ingenuity test. While time-saving appliances are essential, they come in fixed sizes and no amount of wishful thinking can shave off extra centimetres!

So plan! Start with your priorities. How will you use your kitchen? For quick preparation of mainly pre-packed meals? Or are you a keen cook who enjoys home-cooked food? How many people must be catered for? Is entertaining a priority?

Next, list the appliances and utensils you already own and those you intend to buy. Then stand back and study the space available. Start at the door – get rid of it if you can, or install a sliding door to save vital floor space. Can you remove all or part of a wall so that the kitchen opens on to the dining area?

In all probability the majority of kitchen catalogues will set you dreaming but provide little practical help; everything is just a bit too big. You can order specially-designed and built units, but this solution is expensive.

So try a different approach. Buy some boating or caravanning magazines and write off for some of the sales literature on offer. You will be surprised at the space-saving ideas featured in their galleys.

From this study you will learn one critical lesson: everything in your tiny kitchen must have a purpose. There is no room for frills or frippery. But that does not mean that it must be a dreary room. Good design and good planning can make the tiniest kitchen a pleasant and attractive room in which to work.

An open-plan kitchen
Removing the door into a small kitchen saves space. The entrance to this kitchen, which leads on to a dining area, has also been enlarged.

STYLE ON A SMALL SCALE

Aim for clean, open lines in your tiny kitchen so as to create an illusion of greater space. 'Sleek' and 'streamlined' are good descriptions to keep in mind.

Keep colours light: dark wood finishes are fine in a large kitchen but can easily overpower a tiny space. Similarly, decorate the walls to blend rather than contrast with worktops and units. The room will appear larger as a result. Integral doors which fit over appliance fronts (except for cookers) are available in most ranges.

To prevent blandness creeping in, you can highlight the details (such as handles or trims) in contrasting colours.

A fully-tiled kitchen is easy to keep clean — an important consideration as walls tend to get dirtier in a confined space. Avoid tiles with strong patterns — instead choose subtle striped effects or gently-mottled designs. Rectangular tiles laid widthways across a narrow floor will give the appearance of width.

Use lighting to increase the feeling of space: dark corners crowd in on you. Strong overhead lighting is essential but try to avoid casting harsh shadows. Wall-mounted spots concentrate the glow where it is needed and work surfaces can be lit by strip lighting

△ *Sleek and streamlined*
An all-white colour scheme creates clean and simple lines in this narrow, corridor-like kitchen. A space-saving, skirting-board-high central heating radiator warms the room without disturbing the streamlined effect.

hidden beneath wall units.

If your list of priorities includes the need for maximum worktops, covers for the sink and cooker hob can add vital work space. Again, such covers will add to the unbroken surfaces in your tiny kitchen, enhancing that all-important feeling of space.

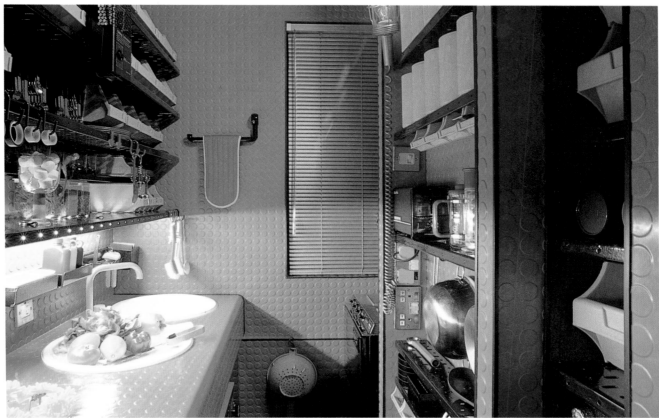

△ Hi-tech kitchen

This kitchen breaks all the rules by using only strong, vibrant colours – apple green, buttercup yellow and vivid red – in a compact room. Although this bright colour scheme may not be to everyone's taste, there is no quibbling with the dramatic effect!

Rubber stud flooring provides an eminently practical worktop and wallcovering. The shelving, constructed from metal and plastic industrial systems, is infinitely flexible.

▷ Simple lines

Finding sufficient storage space is nowhere more important than in a small kitchen. Here, wall units almost to the ceiling make the most of the height of the room, and useful midway units keep spice jars and cooking utensils within easy reach.

STORAGE AND APPLIANCES

Fitting all the basic equipment into a tiny kitchen is a problem in itself; finding space for today's time-saving gadgets as well as a well-stocked larder is a real challenge!

Appliances and fittings A sink of practical dimensions is a must. An empty space-saving sink in a showroom or catalogue can look capacious, but will it hold even a modest number of pots?

If your tiny kitchen is a place for the preparation of quick meals you may well want to include a microwave. A combination oven – the latest microwave technology – can function as both a microwave and a normal convector oven. Some even have two hotplates on top, to replace a cooker hob.

Fridges in tiny kitchens still need to be roomy enough to store sensible quantities of food. Anything less than 133 litres of space is probably only sufficient for one person. Look for a fridge with a 3- or 4-star frozen food compartment. Carefully loaded, a fridge this size will store a surprising amount of food.

You may have to share your tiny kitchen with a washing machine. There's little choice in machine sizes, but most models will fit beneath the draining board. A combined washer/drier saves space. Although a dishwasher will take up valuable space, it is well worthwhile in a tiny kitchen, not least because it provides a place to store dirty dishes.

Time-saving small appliances are always tempting, but they only save time if they are readily to hand and they do occupy valuable worktop space. So keep temptation at bay and settle for the essentials: a food processor, electric kettle and toaster, say.

Storage will be a continual problem and every square centimetre must be utilized. Start by choosing units with pull-out racks, carousels and door-mounted storage space. Assess the height of items to be stored in wall units: extra open shelves can almost always be added to increase storage capacity.

Consider a waste disposal unit in the sink to do away with bulky rubbish bins and look, too, at midway units which store spice jars, mugs and other odds and ends.

Hanging utensils on wall-mounted racks in that midway space is another space-saving idea, leaving cupboards free for less-frequently used items. Ceiling racks are fine if ceilings are high, but they can cause claustrophobia and bumped heads in a room of only average height.

Above all, avoid clutter. Keep only what is absolutely essential near at hand. If you follow this rule your tiny kitchen will serve you well.

△ **A cover for a hob**
Conventional hobs disrupt the continuity of worktops, unless they are placed in a corner. One way of creating an unbroken line of working space is to choose a model which comes with an integral cover. On this electric model, the cover is hinged so that it can easily be pulled down when the hob is not in use.

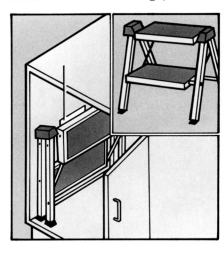

△ **Folding steps**
Steps are essential if the cook is to reach up to high shelves. These sturdy steps come with a fixing bracket so that they can be stored inside a base unit.

△ **Wall-mounting a microwave oven**
A microwave oven can be hung on the wall at a convenient height (using a specially-designed bracket) to free valuable worktop space below.

△ **Tidy cutlery**
A two-tier cutlery drawer such as the one shown here keeps cutlery and utensils tidy and gives you twice the storage space in a single drawer.

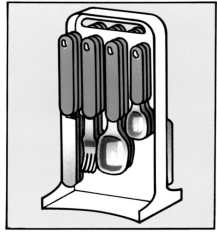

△ **Hanging cutlery**
A cutlery stand can hold a 24-piece cutlery set. Such stands are available in plastic or wood, and the cutlery handles come in various colours.

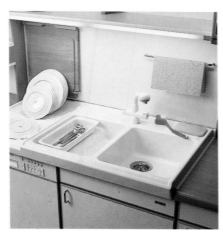

△ **Multi-purpose sink**
This sink incorporates a full-sized bowl and draining board; a second, water-saving stepped bowl; and a drainer which sits across the main bowl (above,

right) or in the upper section of the stepped bowl. A special chopping board can be slotted over the sink or draining board when these are not in use – its lipped edge protects the sink

from damage. To keep worktops uncluttered, the chopping board is stored flat against the wall. (Chopping boards which slot over standard sinks are also available.)

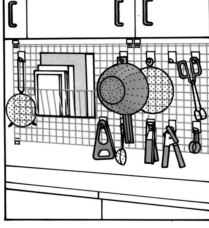
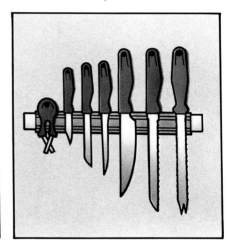

△ **Cup hooks**
Cups and mugs are difficult to stack neatly on a shelf – instead, screw a strip of cup hooks or individual hooks under wall units or in the wall itself.

△ **Wall grid**
Made from strong plastic-coated wire, a wall grid fits into the space between wall and base units to keep utensils – even cookery books – close to hand.

△ **Magnetic knife rack**
A wall-mounted magnetic strip stores kitchen knives neatly, near at hand and safely out of the way. Your knives will keep sharper than if stored in a drawer.

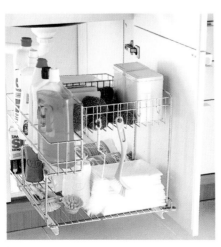

△ **Under-sink storage**
A metal basket which runs on sliding rails fitted to the unit door provides organized storage beneath a sink. Rubber wheels prevent scratching.

△ **A plinth drawer**
This neat, pull-out drawer makes use of the usually dead space in the plinth below base units by providing storage for small, infrequently-used items.

△ **Storage behind cupboard doors**
Pegboard fixed to the inside of a wall unit door can be used to hang utensils from hooks. In larger spaces, special plastic baskets can be used.

WAYS WITH DOORS

Hinged doors, by their very nature, take up space when open and in the tiny kitchen this can be a hazard as well as inconvenient. Dispense with them altogether wherever possible or consider installing sliding or bifold doors.

If you feel you must have a door into the kitchen, try to hinge it so that it opens out of the room. This saves valuable floor space in the kitchen and can prevent an accident if someone enters unexpectedly and bumps into the cook who may be manoeuvring hot pans.

A sliding door is a compromise, but the door must still go somewhere and this requires wall space to house it when open. (Sliding doors for base and wall units are also available.) A better choice might be bifold doors which are hinged down the centre. When opened, the door closes back on itself so that it takes up half the space of a standard door.

▽ Sliding doors
Sliding doors close off this kitchen (and the bathroom behind) and waste minimal space since the doors slide along tracks mounted in the corridor.

△ A folding division
Concertina-style folding doors can be kept fully closed or open, or partially closed to act as a partition between a small kitchen and a dining area.

▽ Bifold cupboard doors
Where sliding doors cannot be installed, bifold doors can provide a space-saving solution since the door can be folded back on itself.

Kitchen Storage

KITCHEN STORAGE CHECKLIST
- ☐ Canned and packet foods
- ☐ Fresh and frozen foods
- ☐ Pots, pans, utensils
- ☐ Electrical equipment
- ☐ Ovenware
- ☐ China and glassware
- ☐ Table linen
- ☐ Cutlery
- ☐ Plastic bags, foil, clingfilm
- ☐ Tea and hand towels
- ☐ Washing up materials
- ☐ Empty jars and bottles
- ☐ Rubbish bin
- ☐ Cleaning materials/implements

Planning kitchen storage can be difficult. All too often, it's a question of trying to fit a quart into a pint pot so start by making a checklist of the items you want to store. This enables you to make the best use of the available space in order to create a tidy, well-ordered kitchen that is a pleasure to use and pleasant to look at.

All in all, there are four basic areas which can provide storage space. Wall units are hung on the walls above work surfaces. The space between these two can be filled with various forms of midway units and shelves. Below the worktop, base units contain cupboard and shelf space, often for bulky or heavy items. And finally, don't forget the ceiling. As long as it's high enough, rarely-used items can generally find a home here.

As a general rule, frequently-used items should be stored close at hand. Things which you use only rarely can be stored high up or low down, but avoid keeping bulky or heavy items too high up, too low down, or in very deep cupboards or shelves.

Combined storage
In a small kitchen, careful planning of storage is essential if everything is to be fitted in. Here a combination of cupboards, drawers and open shelves make use of all the available space. An entire wall fitted with shelves and cup hooks provides a home for decorative and everyday crockery.

△ **A place for everything**
This spacious and streamlined kitchen includes a well-chosen mixture of base and wall units, midway storage space and even a ceiling shelf, as well as several special features.

Look, for example, at the special corner shelves for both base and wall units. These take full advantage of space that might otherwise be lost and they are also rounded so if you bump into them it is less painful.

And doors fitted over the end of the base units in the foreground create a shallow cupboard – for storing spices, perhaps.

THE RIGHT COMBINATION

Whatever the size of your kitchen, careful planning can help you to find a home for everything. In fact, a huge kitchen isn't necessarily an advantage – think of all the extra miles you could clock up during the year! Rather, you should aim to make every single inch of space work to your advantage.

This way, you'll achieve a maximum of storage room without making the room look cluttered or too functional and clinical.

Wall and base units are the backbone of most kitchen storage systems. To accommodate pots and pans as well as small dishes, kitchen units should incorporate a mixture of shelves and drawers, both deep and narrow. Adjustable shelves allow you to change the structure of your storage system over time.
Wall units As most people can reach only the first and second shelves in their wall units, use this area to store everyday china and glass or frequently-used cans and packets of food. The higher shelves can be used for items such as

preserving jars in use only once or twice a year.

It's best to choose wall units which are slightly shallower than the worktop beneath so that you don't hit your head if you lean forward. Cupboards should always be installed over a counter, though, and never over an empty space – the danger of walking into such cupboards is all too real.

Where space is tight, narrow wire shelves can be attached to the back of wall unit doors and used to store small objects. The baskets must be fitted so that they slot into the space between the cupboard shelves when the door is closed. High baskets are difficult to reach into, so use only the lower half of the cupboard door.

Leaving some areas open to view makes the contents easy to get hold of but can mean extra dusting.

A grid system along the wall can incorporate such gadgets as a knife rack, somewhere to hang often-needed utensils, and perhaps even a useful paper towel holder.

◁ **Drip-dry storage**
The old-fashioned scullery idea of having a large built-in plate rack so you just wash up things and pop them straight into their drainage/storage place still has a role to play.

The drainage area is positioned over the sink, and is topped and flanked by open shelving. Cupboards and drawers below the work surface complete the storage system.

▽ **The right mixture**
All the wall units here are slightly shallower than the base units and worktop below. Note how the central shelves are even shallower than their neighbouring cupboards so that extra headroom space is created over the sink. They also make the run of units look less overwhelming.

MIDWAY UNITS

These are designed to make use of the space between worktop and wall units. Most manufacturers offer a range of midways; or you can adapt their ideas.

Wire grids are used with butchers' hooks to hang utensils. Some grid systems are fitted with baskets and shelves. You can make your own cut-price grid by hanging a wire cake cooling tray on the wall.

Hanging rail A chrome or wooden rail suspended under units can be used to hang utensils, wire baskets, sieves and other odds and ends. Make your own rail from a length of dowel or piping.

Shelves Narrow midway shelves are useful for herbs, spices and other frequently-used ingredients. Fix cup hooks under the shelves, or buy some slide-on under-shelf containers to make maximum use of space.

Boxes Manufacturers offer both open and closed midway storage boxes. Some have interior fittings, such as plastic compartments for storing ingredients.

△ A variety of solutions

The planners of this kitchen have incorporated several different types of midway units. Clear plastic storage drawers make it easy to find the right ingredient. Gleaming copper pots hang on a rail above the worktop, and knives are always to hand over the chopping block. A wire rack over the sink completes the range of midway units.

◁ Adding on

Midway units can often be added on to an existing set of wall units. Here ready-made shelves, complete with side brackets, provide a home for condiments, candlesticks and jars. Wooden pegs below can take mugs and cups.

Such shelves can be very narrow. A depth of only about 10cm will take mugs and small jars; wider shelves can hold larger items.

◁ Custom-made shelves

Special-purpose midway storage is relatively easy to construct yourself, although some manufacturers do offer a wide range of units.

Here, a midway shelf houses an electric mixer together with its attachments, as well as a useful cookery book holder.

BELOW THE WORKTOP

Kitchen base units house things of many different shapes and sizes, so it makes sense to have a combination of cupboards, drawers of different depths and open shelves, rather than a uniform row of cupboards and drawers.

Open shelves accommodate pots and pans in daily use, and if you have small children who play in the kitchen, a deep open shelf can hold a toy box. A narrow open space can be used to store serving or baking trays, or fit a telescopic rail for hanging towels.

Base cupboards Pull-out wire baskets mean that you can easily see – and reach – the contents of deep cupboards. There is a storage basket to suit most needs: under-sink baskets, vegetable storage baskets of different sizes, and bottle baskets. Deep shelves are not ideal for base cupboards as objects tend to get pushed to the back.

Corner base units generally incorporate a revolving carousel for storing things in the angle of the corner.

BRIDGE IT

Open shelves sandwiched between closed storage look attractive and are handy for frequently-used utensils.

Some manufacturers include wire trays instead of solid shelves in their range of options. They are also relatively easy to install yourself using metal oven racks.

◁ *Shelve it*
Shelves of standard depth cupboards have to be fairly far apart to enable you to reach objects right at the back. But you can pack as much on to narrow shelves which are spaced closer together to allow for only a single pile of dishes or cups. This way, you gain more floor space.

△ *Below the plinth*
Enterprising kitchen manufacturers use the plinth space beneath base units as a miniature drawer. It is useful for storing tins, baking trays, shoe cleaning materials or a small 'essentials' toolbox containing, perhaps, spare fuses, fuse wire, a screwdriver and torch.

USING THE CEILING

Don't ignore the ceiling in your search for extra storage space. A hanging rack or rail, or a high shelf, can accommodate a surprising number of pots and pans.

Always check that it does not interfere with headroom.

◁ *Room at the top*
Here, utensils not in daily use stand on top of wall units and an extra shelf neatly stores a row of preserve jars. Keep a pair of folding steps handy – don't risk standing on chairs.

▽ *Hanging storage*
A rack suspended by chains from a crossbeam or joist provides valuable extra storage space. Ready-made racks are available, or you can make your own from lengths of piping or broom handles, plus butchers' hooks.

Lighting
the Kitchen

It's a curious fact that while people often spend considerable sums of money on a new fitted kitchen, the lighting of that newly-installed kitchen is often ignored. Yet lighting is possibly more important in a kitchen than elsewhere in the home, partly because of the varied activities that take place there.

Kitchen lighting needs to be conducive to more than just work. The lighting requirements of food preparation differ considerably from those of eating a meal at a kitchen table or breakfast bar. Many families find that their kitchen is the social centre of the home, where members of the family gather to chat and exchange news. Since many hours are spent in the kitchen, good overall lighting will do away with the eye strain and headaches which can be caused by time spent in an environment which is too bright or too dim.

Safety should not be ignored. If you work in your own shadow, or in a room where the level of lighting is too low, you are much more likely to suffer an accidental cut or burn.

Finally, there is the question of aesthetics. A beautiful kitchen cannot look its best if the lighting does not do it justice.

Glowing feel
In this kitchen, a tungsten downlighter provides overall light with a warm, golden quality. Fluorescent strips under the wall units cast bright, shadowless task lighting.

LIGHTING THE WHOLE ROOM

Good overall lighting in a kitchen creates the right mood — neither too bright nor too 'atmospheric' — and produces efficient working conditions.

The level of general lighting which should be installed depends on a combination of factors: the strength of the task lighting, the room's aspect, and whether it is decorated in pale or dark colours. Good natural daylight is a great boon; choose translucent coverings for windows if you need to screen them during the day.

A central strip light, though somewhat utilitarian, provides the best light for the least money. Fluorescent strips (even the modern colour-corrected types) tend to produce a rather harsh, white light which has a 'flattening' effect on fitted furniture; tungsten strips give a yellower, warmer light.

Pendant lights should not throw a glare into the cook's eyes. Match the fittings you choose to the style of the room, bearing in mind that simple shapes which won't act as dirt and grease traps are best in a kitchen.

Spotlights fixed either singly or on a track are flexible as you can angle them more or less where you please. They do create shadows, however, and can cause glare on shiny surfaces.

Downlighters are neat and inconspicuous, particularly if they are recessed into the ceiling. Downlighters direct light

◁ Classic pendant lighting

A series of pendant lamps fitted with classically simple shades provide illumination for the whole room and specific task lighting over the worktops. Such lights need to be carefully positioned: if these lamps were any lower, the cook would be forced to work in a disturbing glare of light.

The single spotlight is fitted with a crown-silvered bulb to reduce glare; it is angled to direct light on to the movable trolley.

▽ Uplighting the kitchen

A pair of elegant tungsten halogen uplighters direct their beams on to the ceiling and bounce light back into the room. Uplighters work on the principle of reflected light so the ceiling must be white or at least pale. Dimmer switches control the light level.

The trolley is lit by a tungsten halogen downlighter. The fitting which has been chosen incorporates a swivel movement allowing the direction of the light to be altered.

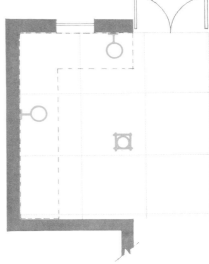

Scale: 1 square = 1 metre square

downwards with a broad or narrow beam, depending on the fitting chosen; some types can be angled.

Wall lights which bounce light off a pale ceiling give good overall illumination and help to avoid shadows. Although tungsten halogen fittings are expensive, the quality of the light they produce is excellent. Since the fittings take very high wattage bulbs, only one or two tungsten halogen uplighters will be needed to light an entire kitchen.

BRIGHT IDEA

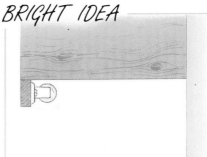

Concealed strip lighting can be installed below wall units or open shelves so that the light, but not the light fitting, is visible. Installing such fittings is one of the easiest ways of improving kitchen lighting. (Either make a baffle to conceal the light or buy one from kitchen specialists.) Fluorescent strips cast very white light; tungsten strips give a warmer and yellower light.

△ *A hand-painted kitchen*
The lighting in this custom-made kitchen, hand-painted in shades of old rose, shows off its delicate lines and glowing colours to advantage.

Concealed tungsten strip lighting below the wall units provides task lighting and casts a warm, yellowish glow. (Fluorescent strips would give off a colder, whiter light and would make the delicate pink appear bluer in colour.) Recessed downlighters fitted into the ceiling provide inconspicuous overall lighting; the gold-effect reflectors enhance the warm quality of the light.

▷ *Varied lighting*
A combination of fluorescent strips and tungsten downlighters light this all-white kitchen.

Fitted both below and above the wall units, fluorescent strips throw a white light down on to the work surfaces (including the sink) and upwards on to the ceiling. The ribbon of light around the top of the room which the strips create adds a definite touch of drama. The recessed tungsten downlighter lights the rest of the room.

◁ **Modern and streamlined**
Concealed tungsten strip lighting above and below the wall units casts a yellowish glow on to worktops and ceiling, balancing the cool colour of the kitchen units. The miniature eyeball-type recessed downlighters sparkle and glitter, but leave the floor in relative darkness. Neither the hidden strips nor the downlighters disturb the streamlined look of the room.

TASK LIGHTING

Efficient kitchen lighting must be shadow-free. This means that any task lighting you install must be positioned so that you do not stand between the light source and the worktop, so casting shadows. Beware, also, of the glare which can be caused by bouncing over-bright light off shiny tiles, worktops and appliances. Either direct the light away from reflective surfaces, or use lower wattage bulbs.

So long as there are wall units (or shelves) above the worktops, the best way of providing task lighting is to install strip lights beneath. But if your kitchen has no fitted wall units, suspend a number of pendant lamps over the worktops. Positioning them above the outside edge of the worktop will ensure that you cast no shadow as you work. Alternatively, one or more angled work lamps on a shelf or the worktop itself provide good task lighting.

Even if the sink is located beneath a window, it will need its own light source. A downlighter on the ceiling should do the job well (it's best to avoid spotlights since they produce a very strong, glaring light). Another alternative is to install hidden lighting behind a pelmet. Similarly, the hob needs a separate light source. Many cooker hoods incorporate an integral light; if you need to install a light, choose a fitting in which the bulb or strip is enclosed to protect it from heat and grease splashes.

▽ **Alternative arrangement**
The two large recessed downlighters which replace miniature eyeballs in this lighting scheme ensure that light reaches the rather dark floor. They throw a wide beam and so create two overlapping pools of light.

An additional strip light installed below the display shelves highlights the collection of ornaments. It has been hidden behind a baffle (painted to match the walls) for safety as well as style.

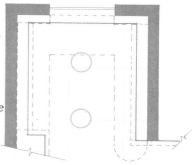

Scale: 1 square = 1 square metre

LIGHTING A DINING AREA

The lighting in a kitchen which includes a dining area must be flexible enough to create the right atmosphere for meals.

The simplest arrangement is to make sure that one of the light fittings used for general illumination is positioned above the table. A pendant lamp will emphasize the eating area, and the type of fitting you choose will set the style of the dining area.

It's best to arrange for the dining table lighting to be switched independently or to have a dimmer switch fitted so that the overall lighting level, particularly in the kitchen area, can be reduced at mealtimes.

▷ *Farmhouse style*
An elaborate pendant lamp, in the style of an oil-lamp, turns this dining table into the room's focal point. The remainder of the lighting is provided by inconspicuous recessed downlighters and under-cupboard tungsten strips.

▽ *A kitchen/diner*
A modern pendant lamp highlights the dining table in a large kitchen and yet remains in keeping with the style of the rest of the lighting. The lamp is suspended from a rise-and-fall fitting so that it can be lowered for formal meals and raised for family dinners.

Work Surfaces and Splashbacks

Since kitchen worktops have to bear the brunt of most cooking activity, they must be able to withstand the heavy wear and tear that they will be subjected to without becoming shabby or grubby. Although splashbacks don't need to be quite so hardwearing, they should nevertheless be easy to clean.

Even if you always use a chopping board, a worktop will occasionally be subjected to nicks and scratches. So the surface must be strong and resilient. It also needs to be able to withstand at least moderate heat to prevent burn marks if a hot pan is put down on it.

And since you are bound to spill things on it, the ideal worktop is also easy to clean, stain-resistant and waterproof.

Lastly, worktops and splashbacks should be as attractive as possible since they are an important element in any kitchen design.

The dimensions Standard base units are 900mm in height since this is judged to be the most comfortable height for most people. But if you are taller or shorter than average, some kitchen manufacturers can alter the height of the plinth in order to raise or lower the worktop accordingly.

The normal depth of base units (from front to back) is 600mm and the worktop is usually a few centimetres deeper. It is possible to install a deeper worktop by positioning base units a small distance from the wall. This gives more room to range toasters, electric kettles and similar appliances neatly along the back wall without encroaching on work space – and also means that pipes can be hidden behind the units.

Materials Kitchen worktops can be made from many different materials, with differing visual and practical characteristics and, of course, different prices. The most common materials are plastic laminates, wood and ceramic tiles. Granite, marble and man-made materials which resemble natural stone are also available.

Farmhouse style

Wooden worktops and a tiled splashback provide practical surfaces which are in keeping with the natural style of this kitchen. A butcher's block acts as a chopping board and a marble slab on top of the worktop provides a cool surface for rolling out pastry.

PLASTIC LAMINATES

By far the most popular choice for kitchen worktops, plastic laminates are available in an overwhelming variety of colours and effects. These range from pale pastels to bright primaries, through imitations of natural materials such as wood and marble – even bold geometric patterns.

A plastic laminate is made up of a thin sheet of plastic bonded to chipboard, blockboard or plywood (in ascending order of quality and price). Formica is the brand name of one of the best known ranges of plastic laminates. Melamine is a cheaper alternative to plastic laminate and is made from plastic-impregnated paper.

Most fitted kitchen manufacturers offer a selection of laminate worktops to co-ordinate with their range of units, but laminate can also be bought separately in cut lengths for DIY kitchen fitting, or to replace an existing worktop.

Although boiling water and hot splashes will do no harm, a hot pan or iron should never be placed directly on to a laminate worktop. Similarly, laminates are generally resistant to knocks and scratches, but should never be used as a chopping surface.

△ **Cream and blue**
It is almost always possible to co-ordinate the plastic laminate worktops with the units in a fitted kitchen. A single line of patterned tiles on the splashback make a visual link with the grey-blue trim on the units.

▽ **Spoilt for choice**
The plastic laminate worktops shown below – speckled grey, plain pink and wood-effect – are just three of the huge variety available. The edge of the worktop can be square (in this case cleverly accentuated with a darker pink inset stripe) or curved.

CERAMIC AND QUARRY TILES

While most ordinary ceramic tiles can be used for kitchen worktops, tiles manufactured specially for this purpose will last longer. Quarry tiles, designed to be laid on floors, are also suitable and create a rugged, rustic feel. Although worktop and quarry tiles are thicker than ordinary ceramic wall tiles, they can be fixed to walls to create a co-ordinated splashback.

Look for ranges which include curved edging tiles for a neat finish. (Some manufacturers even produce mitred edging tiles for the corners.) Alternatively, a wooden edging will neatly frame worktop tiling.

Tiles are very easy to keep clean, are not easily scratched and are less likely to be damaged by hot saucepans than many other worktop materials.

A tiled worktop is noisy to work on. In addition, individual tiles can be chipped or cracked if something heavy is accidentally dropped, though this is less likely to happen with quarry or purpose-made worktop tiles. Replacing a single tile can be difficult.

Tiles can be laid over an existing – perhaps disfigured – worktop but it is important to ensure that the existing worktop is strong enough to take the weight of the tiles. If it is not adequately supported, a tiled worktop can begin to sag.

Grouting Since the tiles on a worktop are laid on a horizontal rather than a vertical surface, water is liable to collect on the surface, particularly in the grouting which is usually slightly recessed. This means that waterproof grouting is essential to prevent water seeping into the surface below the tiles. It is also important to ensure that there are no gaps between the tiles and the grouting, where crumbs and similar bits could collect.

Grouting can, with time, get very grubby and needs to be regularly cleaned with a stiff brush and a solution of domestic bleach. It may occasionally be necessary to rake out the existing grouting and replace it. White grouting has a tendency to go grey, so an off-white or coloured grouting may be worth considering.

MAN-MADE STONE

Although the various synthetic materials now available for kitchen worktops feel like smooth stone and can look like marble or granite, they suffer from none of their disadvantages (except price). Corian (the best-known man-made stone) is virtually indestructible – it is hardwearing, warm to the touch and completely heat and stain resistant. Small scratches are easily removed by rubbing down with ordinary kitchen cleaner. It can be moulded into almost any shape, to create an integral worktop, sink and draining board with no joins in which dirt and germs can hide. However, it is very expensive.

▽ *Shades of pink*
A tiled worktop and splashback add colour and interest to this all-white kitchen. The large expanse of tiles is broken up by mixing various shades of pink on the worktop and combining white and pink tiles and a border with a fuchsia design on the splashback. Grey grouting complements the pink tiles and won't discolour and look shabby.

WOOD, GRANITE AND MARBLE

These natural materials all produce elegant and attractive, though expensive, worktops.

Wood A wooden worktop is best made from a hardwood – teak, maple, oak and beech are common choices. Some wooden worktops are sealed with a clear varnish; others are treated with a special oil which must be periodically renewed. The types of wood used for worktops is hardwearing and will withstand moderate heat although very hot pans may scorch the surface. A tiled inset next to a hob or oven can be used for standing hot pans.

Solid wood comes in different thicknesses (and therefore different qualities); wood veneer (where a thin sheet of real wood is bonded to chipboard or hardboard) represents a cheaper alternative which can be equally longlasting.

Marble and granite are undoubtedly elegant and virtually indestructible – but are also very expensive and heavy, so that the units (and the floor) may need to be reinforced in order to be able to bear the weight. Marble is porous and should be coated with a special sealant to help prevent it staining with alarming ease. Granite is less porous and also comes as a veneer.

△ **Granite splendour**
There is no arguing with the fact that the granite worktop and splashback add a touch of opulence to this kitchen. The shiny, mottled grey surface goes well with bright primary colours. Granite comes in a variety of colours which include dark and light greys as well as shades of green and pink. While some granites are very mottled, in others the colour is more solid.

◁ **A maple worktop**
Tough enough to be used for squash courts and dance floors, solid maple is an ideal choice for a worktop. Treated with respect, wood actually improves with age and use, unlike plastic laminate or tiles.

A custom-made wood worktop can replace an existing damaged worktop – or add the finishing touch to a new kitchen. The worktop's edge can be square, rounded or even chamfered – depending on your preference.

SPLASHBACKS

As the name implies, the splashback area above the worktop must be easy to clean so that splashes and spills from cooking can be removed without causing lasting damage.

The choice of material depends partly on your choice of worktop and kitchen units. Ceramic wall or worktop tiles, quarry tiles, laminates – even marble and granite – are all suitable.

In addition, of course, a splashback can be painted or covered with wallpaper. Although it is fairly easy to renew paint and wallpaper, it's best to use an oil-based paint or a washable wallpaper to give a reasonably longlasting finish. Instead of tiles, consider a tile-effect washable wallpaper which to all intents and purposes looks very like real tiles.

Visually, the worktop and splashback should not be equally dominant or the end result could be overwhelming. A bright or highly patterned splashback is best combined with a plain or pale worktop, and vice versa. Remember too that strong patterns – on either the worktop or the splashback – may conflict with the many utensils which find a home on most kitchen worktops, so creating a working environment which is over-busy and distracting.

△ *A personal splashback*
In a farmhouse-style kitchen, a fully-tiled splashback may look out of place. Here, a small tiled area of Victorian tiles framed in wood, provides a practical and sympathetic backdrop to an old, marble-topped sideboard.

Odd tiles, as opposed to a complete set in the same pattern, are easy to find in antique shops and markets. Choose tiles which have a theme – or a colour – in common.

▷ *Chequerboard effect*
Combined with plain units and worktops, an eye-catching splashback can form the visual focus of a kitchen.

Here, a simple arrangement of black and white tiles is reminiscent of the op art so popular during the 1960s.

A softer effect could be produced by using more subdued colours or patterned tiles.

A pull-out table can fit snugly into a drawer space and slide out to extend the available worktop space. Such an extendable surface could also double as a tea tray or occasional breakfast table.

When you choose a pull-out table, check that it is securely supported along its entire length when extended.

MAKING WORKTOP SPACE

Except for those lucky enough to possess an exceptionally large kitchen, most cooks would agree that they have insufficient worktop space for their needs. The most costly solution is to rearrange completely the entire room in order to squeeze in as much worktop space as possible. But there are less drastic solutions.

Start by trying to free as much of the existing worktops as possible. Rows of storage jars or tins may look attractive ranged along the back wall, but they do take up valuable space. Small appliances such as food processors can often be stored in cupboards rather than on worktops. Some kitchen manufacturers even offer pull-out shelves which allow appliances to be stored behind closed doors.

If there is room, a movable trolley can serve as an additional worktop (as well as providing extra storage) – but choose a version with locking wheels for safety. You may even be able to purchase an old butcher's block with a solid wood top which makes an ideal chopping board.

△ **A movable trolley**
A trolley with locking castors provides an extra worktop which can be moved out of the way when not in use.

▽ **Using the walls**
A spare wall can be made to work for its living by means of a securely fixed, collapsible shelf.

Colour in the Kitchen

Creating a pleasing colour scheme for a kitchen can be more complicated than for any other room in the home as there are so many elements to consider. And kitchens generally contain expensive appliances and fitted units which cannot be replaced at a whim.

Fitted units come in a whole host of colours and finishes, ranging from the highly dramatic to the subtle. And since coloured facing panels are now available for many kitchen appliances, a degree of colour co-ordination can be achieved between appliances and units as well as surfaces such as walls and ceiling.

Kitchens contain, too, many small appliances and utensils that are always on show. If too many colours or patterns are involved, the result is bitty, busy and tiring on the eye.

The room's size and aspect always influence the colours chosen. A small, dark room benefits from light, airy colours and – in addition – the smaller the room, the greater the risk of fragmentation – so use plain, uninterrupted colours for a streamlined look.

These are just some of the considerations to bear in mind when planning your kitchen. Choose colours and patterns for the long term and – as you decide on the main colours – remember to consider the accessories which will add the finishing touches.

Fresh and simple
The colour of the wooden units in this kitchen is lifted by the crisp white contrast and a judicious use of clear primaries. The resulting atmosphere is both cheerful and relaxed.

LARGE AREAS OF COLOUR

When choosing the main colours or patterns which will predominate in your kitchen, it's a good idea to start with the fitted units and worktops. Then consider the elements that can be changed more easily and cheaply – wall and floorcoverings, or paintwork (and, of course, the accessories and details).

Apart from your personal preferences and the mood you're aiming for, be sure you can live with your choice over the years. A good choice, for instance, is fitted units in neutral white, beiges and creams, or natural wood.

The amount of daylight is an important consideration. Pale colours reflect light and can make a room feel larger, but too much white could be dazzling in a sunny, south-facing kitchen.

▷ *Formal stripes*
Strong patterns don't look their best broken up by shelves or racks, so keep them away from work areas – like this striped wallpaper above the wall units.

▽ *Coloured units*
Moss green kitchen units create a restrained background in this room. Stained floorboards, a rug and matching seating complete the co-ordinated look.

△ **Hand-painted units**
Wooden kitchen units can be painted almost any colour under the sun: here a warm cornflower blue with white detailing has been chosen. The dragged paint effect is protected by several coats of clear varnish to provide a longlasting finish.

The white, tiled worktop and splashback and the blue and white patterned blind emphasize the scheme.

◁ **High-tech look**
Glossy black kitchen units create a streamlined, modern look with the pale wood trim on the units adding a subtle note of relief to the stark black. Neutral walls and worktops, together with a black floor, complete the overall scheme.

COLOUR IN THE DETAILS

The kitchen, with small worktop appliances, utensils, storage pots and jars, table linen and crockery, affords great scope for using small areas of colour to highlight and break up the large expanses of worktops and units. Planning is important, however, both to stop the room becoming too busy and to prevent colourful accessories clashing with each other.

Having decided on the main colours for the room, choose accessories which blend or contrast with the overall scheme. If the background is pale and unobtrusive so that the main colour interest lies in the accesssories, try to select at least a couple of larger items in the accent colour of your choice – tiles, perhaps, or the tablecloth or window covering.

Then colour match the rest of the room's details as far as possible to avoid a fragmented look. Paint door and window frames to blend with the colour scheme. Although it may be difficult to find small electrical appliances in identical colours, you should be able to find complementary shades or discreet neutrals. Light fittings, pots and pans, chopping boards, oven gloves, tea towels, mugs on racks, the cutlery and crockery – even the kitchen sink – can all add to your colour scheme.

△ ◁ *A whole new look*
The two kitchens shown here (above and left) are structurally identical, and have the same layout, fitted units and dining table. The difference lies in the clever use of coloured detailing that totally transforms the look of the room.

The kitchen above is enlivened by using plenty of red and white – from the wallpaper to the floor and a range of accessories.

In the kitchen on the left, a soft and sophisticated colour scheme has been created by retaining the same units and combining them with delicate pastel shades throughout the room.

▷ *Bold primaries*
Some kitchen units allow you to choose from different coloured handles and trims above and below wall and base units. The glossy yellow ceiling echoes the colour of the window frame and reflects the plentiful natural light in the room.

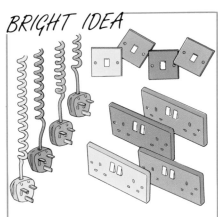

◁ *Blue outline*
Simple white units are given a smart new look with a neat blue trim. To achieve this effect yourself, use masking tape to protect the surrounding surface when painting existing units.

◁ *Open shelves*
It is possible to brighten up a rather dull kitchen at minimal expense, simply by painting the walls. And paint is inexpensive and easy to renew if you feel like a change in the future.

Here blue and white china, together with a variety of kitchen necessities, are arranged on open shelves against a pillar-box red background. By choosing the colours carefully, the china and crockery displayed on open shelves make an important contribution to the overall look of a kitchen.

▽ *A painted kitchen*
In a kitchen which lacks fitted wall units, it is easy to introduce colour by painting the walls. Do beware, though, of creating an overpowering atmosphere if you opt for a strong colour. Here, for example, touches of red and brown break up the large expanses of green and tie in well with the cherry motif on the curtains.

Streamlining Kitchen Gaps

FITTING ON A BUDGET

Problem When installing a fitted kitchen, a limited budget can make it impossible to afford the number of fitted base units needed. How can the kitchen be made to look fitted and streamlined without filling all the space with expensive units?

Solution Use a combination of fitted units and open shelves. Space the closed units to suit your needs, then fill up the spaces in between with inexpensive shelving. Contiboard comes in white, wood effect, primary and pastel colours.

You can even leave some gaps the width of a standard base unit. This allows you to insert a unit when you can afford it. Alternatively, choose a range where doors can be bought separately and simply cover the open shelves with doors when your budget allows.

Open shelves between units can be used in many different ways. Two deep shelves provide room on the bottom for a beer crate with a wine rack on top. Wire or wicker baskets can be used on narrow shelves for convenient and easily-accessible storage.

SPACE FOR TOWELS OR TRAYS

Problem What can be done with a narrow space too small for a kitchen unit?

Solution Gaps, at the end of kitchen units, or between them on a wall, that are the wrong length to accommodate an exact number of standard units are irritating and a waste of space.

You can use the gap to house trays, or you can buy a custom-made fitting to fill the space.

The most useful fitting is a telescopic towel rail. These are available with two or three arms. The rail can be fixed beneath the work surface above the gap, or to the back wall. The rails pull forward so that towels are easy to reach.

Another way to fill the space is to buy a set of folding kitchen steps. These measure around 90mm wide when folded and will slide into a narrow under-worktop space. It is also possible to buy steps which fit behind a removable section of the base plinth.

Alternatively, fit shelves across the gap and use them to store small jars of spices and other kitchen odds and ends.

△ *Adding an eating area*
A simple breakfast bar can be used to fill space between units or across the end of the room. A length of work surface makes a good, solid top.

ADD A BREAKFAST BAR

Problem What is the best way to deal with a long gap if you can't afford to fit units?

Solution Run a worktop or a narrow shelf across the gap and add a couple of stools to create an instant breakfast bar. If you want to make use of the space beneath the worktop, fill it with wine racks (available made-to-measure from good cookshops and some wine merchants), stacking plastic boxes or tiers of wire trays on castors.

You can link units across the end wall of a room by running a narrow breakfast bar between them. This works particularly well if the bar can be positioned beneath a window. Eating breakfast or a snack facing a blank wall is less appealing. The area beneath the bar must be left open so that the unit doors can be used.

◁ *Using open spaces*
Spaces can be filled with shelves at different depths to house a mixture of objects. Spacing units out with open shelf areas is a useful exercise if you can't afford as many cupboards as you would like.

◁ ***Filling the gaps***
Gaps beside a cooker or between units can be filled with a useful telescopic towel rail. The rails are available from flat pack kitchen unit suppliers. You can buy a rail with a heating element to dry the tea towels. This type of rail must be fitted by an electrician.

MIDWAY STORAGE

Problem In a kitchen where storage space is limited, it seems wasteful not to use the area between the worktop and the wall units. What kind of fitting can be used here without obstructing the worktop space?

Solution Fitting baskets to the underside of wall cupboards doesn't obstruct the space below. Under-shelf baskets are available made from plastic-covered wire mesh with open fronts, or from rigid plastic with up-and-over doors. The up-and-over door type is useful for storing bread, biscuits and other perishables which need protection from the drying effect of air.

Cup hooks fixed beneath units are useful for hanging mugs and bunches of dried herbs. If your greatest need is for hanging storage, fix metal mesh grids to the wall between the units and the worktop. Use butchers' hooks to hang utensils from the racks. Some racks feature a range of accessories, such as hook-on baskets for cleaning materials, shelves and a circular container to hold washing-up liquid. These are useful above the sink.

Narrow shelves are another way to use the wall space. The shelves should be a maximum of 15cm (6in) wide and must finish at least 25cm (10in) above the worktop. Shelves wider or lower than this obstruct the worktop. Use the shelves for spice jars and other small containers.

GAPS AROUND THE COOKER

Problem Old cookers were not designed to fit in with modern kitchen units so there are often narrow gaps at each side. How can these gaps be filled to give a neat, streamlined look?

Solution Gaps beside the cooker are a collecting point for crumbs and food spills. You can fill the space with a piece of worktop, mounted on a batten at one side (the batten can be fixed to the wall or unit next to the gap) and hard up against the side of the cooker at the other side. This prevents food and crumbs falling into the gap.

The space below the worktop can be used as a tray recess, for a telescopic towel rail or filled with shelves for storing spices and other ingredients.

SPACE BETWEEN WALL UNITS

Problem Where a kitchen has been fitted in a haphazard way, with units at different levels and spaces between them the effect is visually disturbing and untidy. How can this higgeldy-piggeldy arrangement be given a neat, streamlined look, without fitting a completely new range of units?

Solution Where there are several units mounted at different levels, the easiest way to bring them together is to run a shelf across the top. The shelf should be positioned just above the highest unit. Use the shelf to display an attractive collection of jugs, pots or bowls and you'll draw the eye away from the cupboards. Run a second shelf across the bottom, starting beneath the lowest unit. Running shelves across top and bottom creates interesting spaces which can be used for display. You can attach cup hooks to the underside of the bottom shelf and use them for hanging mugs, jugs and utensils.

Wall cupboards can be linked by running open shelves between them. Space shelves wide apart for pans and other large objects, close together for spice jars and odds and ends.

▽ ***Space between units***
Spaces between both wall and floor units can be filled with open shelves set at different depths. Use shallow baskets on the shelves to keep small items in order and easily accessible.

△ ***Around the cooker***
Narrow spaces around and above this cooker have been filled with open shelving to give a streamlined look.

LINING UP NEATLY

Problem Modern appliances are all a standard 600mm deep (front to back). If used with old style 500mm kitchen units, they jut out, spoiling the line of the units and causing awkward gaps.

Solution The easiest way to deal with this problem is to remove the worktop from the old units. Move the units forward, so that they line up with the appliances, then fit a new 600mm deep worktop to cover the gap at the back.

You won't be able to do this where an appliance is next to the sink as it would involve moving the water pipes and drains, but one area set back does not look as untidy as a wall of zig-zags. If you have a gas cooker, the supply pipe must be extended. This should be done by a gas fitter.

Basic Fitted Kitchen Units

A fitted kitchen means that all or nearly all available space is used for storage, with no obvious gaps between units. It is a dramatic contrast to the old-fashioned type of kitchen which might have a sink, a table, a cooker, a refrigerator and one or two cupboards – all as separate items. A fully-fitted kitchen consists of matching wall and floor cupboards, incorporating a sink and oven with electrical appliances under a continuous worktop. (The most popular choice of cooking appliances in this type of kitchen is a split-level oven/grill in a tall housing unit and a separate hob set into a base unit.)

Base units The basis of a fitted kitchen is the base unit. This is usually 600mm deep (from front to back) and 600mm wide (side to side). This is known as the standard 600mm module.

Domestic appliances are now made to fit the 600mm module size as well, but when planning you often need to allow for a slight gap for washing machines and tumble driers (for vibration) and for refrigerators and free-standing cookers (for air circulation).

Apart from the 600mm module, there are many variations in size. For example, you can buy single base units 200mm, 300mm, 400mm and 500mm wide, double base units 1000mm or 1200mm wide, or triple width base units 1500 to 1800mm wide. These are all generally 600mm deep.

Once you have the basic unit you then need a worktop to go on top and a plinth for the units to stand on. The plinth is usually 100 or 150mm high although you can get lower or higher plinths if you are particularly short or tall. Once assembled, the unit (generally 850mm high) will give you a working area of around 900mm in height. Base units are floorstanding but should also be screwed to the wall and to each other.

Tall units These also stand on the floor, but are taller – designed to be used as broom cupboards, larder units or for housing appliances, especially split-level ovens. A typical tall unit suitable as larder/broom cupboard or for housing an oven stands around 2000mm high (600mm wide, 600mm deep).

Wall units should be fixed to the wall above the worktop and are generally around half the depth of base units so you don't hit your head on them when using the work surface below. They are available in widths and heights from 200-1000mm. Before buying wall units decide whether you want them to go right up to the ceiling – taller units are usually more expensive, whereas standard units may leave you with wasted space above.

If you have tall units in your kitchen, standard wall units are generally positioned so that all the tops line up. If there are no tall cupboards, you need a gap of about 450mm between the top of the worktop and the bottom of the wall units – for practicality's sake.

Both base and wall units come in versions which fit into a corner.

Materials There is a wide choice of materials for kitchen units. Generally, the carcases and shelves of units are made from chipboard faced with melamine. Doors and drawer fronts (fascias) and sometimes the exposed end panels are made of other decorative materials:
☐ Solid wood (mainly pine and oak, but other woods available).
☐ Wood veneer (thin wood strips glued to chipboard – less expensive than solid wood, but similar in finished appearance).
☐ Wood/plastic laminate mixture (mainly white, coloured or textured melamine laminate with wood trims and handles).
☐ Plastic laminate (white or coloured, plain, textured or wood-effect) such as melamine or the popular brand Formica. There are also lacquer, polyester and other special finishes.

Worktops Chipboard faced with plastic laminate is the most popular choice, but other options include hardwood, ceramic tiles, quarry tiles, granite, marble, or a solid man-made stone-like material such as Corian.

BASE UNITS

   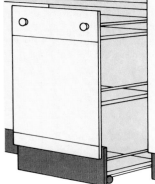

STANDARD UNITS
Style Floorstanding cupboards with one, two or three doors depending on the width of the unit.
In use Base units come in two styles – plain and drawerline. Plain units have full-height doors; drawerline units have drawers at the top. Single unit doors can be hinged on the left

or the right.
Watchpoint High-quality units offer a choice of shelf positions, unit bottoms are coated with a sealant to prevent moisture swelling the chipboard, adjustable feet keep the carcase off the floor and there are additional supports in the centre of long shelves.

DRAWER UNITS
Style Available in the same sizes as standard units, drawer units consist entirely of drawers.
In use A good number of drawers in a kitchen is useful and a drawer unit should always be incorporated especially if plain – no drawerline – base units are used. Most

drawer units have three or four drawers; pan drawers have two deep drawers – the whole unit including drawers, fascia, and sometimes the plinth fascia too, pulls out for maximum access – particularly suited for storing saucepans.
Watchpoint Check that the drawers open and close smoothly.

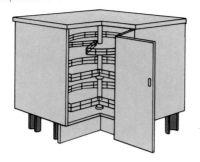

L-shaped corner unit

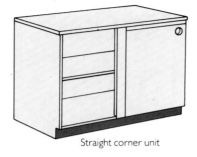

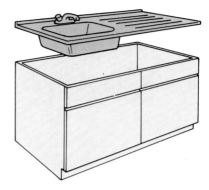

Straight corner unit

CORNER UNITS

Style A base unit which is designed to fit into a corner between two meeting runs of units.

In use There are two types of corner unit. The L-shaped corner unit has open shelves or a double-hinged door so the entire contents of the shelves can be seen. Often fitted with swing-out shelves. Alternatively there is a straight corner unit. This is a double unit with only one door – the other half of the unit is just open shelves. The adjacent units then fit against the open half. With the shelf removed, this type of corner cupboard is often fitted with a carousel (see opposite).

SINK UNITS

Style A unit for a kitchen sink.

In use Sit-on sink/drainers (usually stainless steel) are designed to sit directly on one of these units. Such a sink also incorporates a lip which runs along the front of the unit and a narrow 'splashback' along the back. A sink unit doesn't usually have a central shelf, as the space is needed for the plumbing. A drawerline sink unit has only one real drawer under the drainer, plus a dummy drawer in front of the bowl.

TALL UNITS

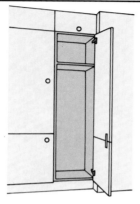

Pull-out larder unit

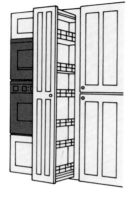

BROOM CUPBOARDS

Style A tall cupboard for storing cleaning equipment.

In use Broom cupboards are generally 300-600mm wide and may incorporate one or two shelves and have one or two doors. Usually tall enough for brooms and mops and often used for storing vacuum cleaners and small kitchen steps.

Watchpoint Some have two doors which both have to be opened to take out large items.

LARDER UNITS

Style A tall cupboard used for storing food.

In use Some look like a broom cupboard – only the shelves are closer together. Others are pull-out larder units which have wire racks attached to the door fascia so the whole interior slides out on runners.

Watchpoint They don't usually have any vents in them for fresh air to circulate, so should not be used for perishable food.

APPLIANCE HOUSING UNITS

Style A tall cupboard for domestic appliances – typically single or double ovens.

In use Although you can get housing units for 'single' ovens to 'slide under' a worktop, most people opt for a tall unit – 600mm wide – to take a single or double oven (and perhaps a microwave) so they are positioned further off the ground. Cupboards above and below the appliance provide space for storing pots and pans.

WALL UNITS

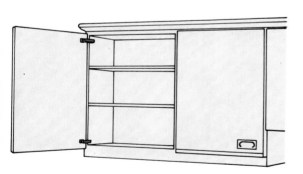

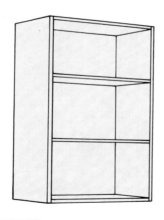

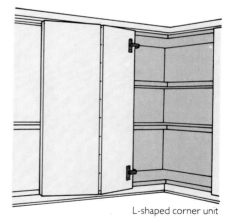

L-shaped corner unit

STANDARD UNITS

Style The standard wall unit is a single or double cupboard 500mm or 1000mm wide, fitted with one or two shelves and doors (plain or glazed).

In use Two heights of wall cupboard are generally available – standard (600mm high to match the tops of tall wall units) and extra-height (900mm), which are suitable to go right up to the ceiling. As with base units, other widths are available and single-unit doors can open either way.

OPEN SHELVES

Style Plain shelves designed to be installed in a run of wall units. Rounded shelves for the end of a run of units are another option.

In use They are also available with gallery rails which not only look decorative, but are also handy to secure display plates and special tableware.

CORNER UNITS

Style A wall unit that is designed to fit into a corner between two adjacent runs of units.

In use As with base corner units, two styles are available – straight and L-shaped.

Watchpoint Check which way the cupboard doors open and whether this is going to be convenient and safe in use.

Kitchen Unit Extras

Once your kitchen layout has been designed and the base, wall and tall units chosen, there is a whole range of extras which can be fitted in, on or under the basic units to make a kitchen easier or more efficient to use.

Most of these extras are additional compartments for storage of one sort or another; racks, drawers, bins, and so on. Others are hide-away fitments, such as ironing boards, tables, mixer support plinths or book rests.

Even matching cornices and pelmets are available to provide the finishing touches to your kitchen.

EXTRAS FOR BASE UNITS

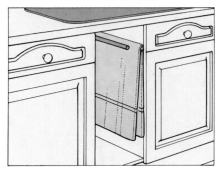

TOWEL RAILS
Style The odd gap or space between cupboards in a run of base units is almost inevitable. Make use of this space by fitting a telescopic towel rail to the underside of the worktop over the space.
In use Ideally this should be positioned as close to the sink as possible.

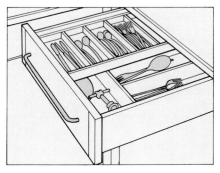

CUTLERY TRAYS
Style All ranges of kitchen units offer divided cutlery tray inserts to fit into drawers.
In use This helps you keep cutlery neat and tidy. Look out for the double-decker inserts – these are two-tier, allowing you to store twice as much without everything becoming jumbled together.

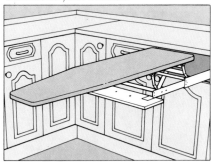

IRONING BOARDS
Style A pull-out ironing board for *in situ* ironing, hidden behind a dummy drawer-front.
In use Not usually as large or as easy to use as a freestanding ironing board.

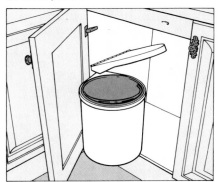

WASTE BINS
Style In a fitted kitchen, there is often no space for a separate waste bin. A fitted bin positioned on the back of a cupboard door opens automatically when the door is opened. There is also one which fits into a deep drawer.
In use Takes up space within a cupboard.

BASKETS
Style There are many types of wire baskets and racks which fit on to the back of opening cupboard doors or into the cupboard itself.
In use Choose from those which hang like shelves, pull-out on runners like drawers, or just stack.

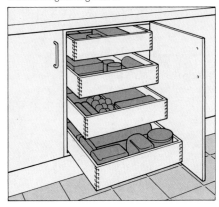

PULL-OUTS
Style A door-fronted unit which has all-wood, old-fashioned drawers – called pull-outs – in it.
In use These are much more expensive than ordinary drawer units.

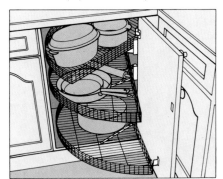

CAROUSELS
Style A semi-circular, plastic-coated wire tray which fits on the inside of the opening door of a straight corner cupboard.
In use Generally more suited to storing things which are light in weight.

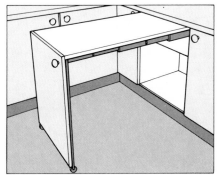

PULL-OUT TABLES
Style There are various styles. This one fits behind a dummy door fitted with castors. The whole unit pulls out on telescopic rails.
In use Provides a useful table or extra surface, pulls out to a maximum of the worktop's width.

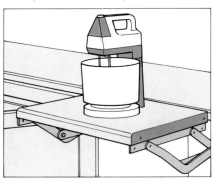

MIXER SUPPORTS
Style Full-size table mixers can be extremely heavy to get out of a cupboard.
In use A mixer support provides a solution – this is a spring-loaded table which swings up for use and away again into the base unit.

WINE STORAGE
Style Wine racks are often available as alternatives to base units.
In use Typically, one rack fits into a 300mm space – two fit side-by-side in a unit. Bottles are stored on their sides.

DECOR PANELS
Style Many appliances, such as dishwashers and fridges can be fitted with these fronts so that they blend in with rest of kitchen units.
In use They clip over the appliance's existing doors. Decor panels are only available for certain ranges of fitted kitchens.

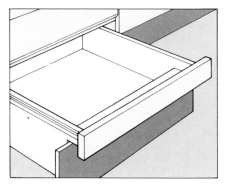

PLINTH DRAWERS
Style Special drawers which fit into the space under kitchen units.
In use Ideal for under-oven storage for baking tins and roasting trays.
Also look out for a neat two-step ladder which fits into the plinth space – excellent for reaching high wall cupboards.

OPEN SHELVES
Style A rounded open-shelving unit that fits at the end of a run of units.
In use These provide additional storage as well as being a neat way of finishing off the run.

SMALLER DETAILS
When planning a kitchen, don't forget to consider future requirements for the services and the smaller accessories which add the finishing touches.
- ☐ With the number of appliances in an average kitchen, it is a good idea wherever possible to have a separate socket circuit for the kitchen.
- ☐ Fit as many socket outlets as possible – certainly no less than eight (four doubles) for an average-size kitchen – not including switched spur outlets for fixed appliances such as an electric cooker.
- ☐ Under-cupboard lights to illuminate worksurfaces.
- ☐ Cooker hoods or extractor fans.
- ☐ Dummy drawer fronts to conceal pull-out fittings such as ironing boards or foldaway tables or to disguise gaps between units.
- ☐ Cornicing and architraves to match your units.
- ☐ Extras for worktops such as inset sinks or hobs, ceramic tile inserts for hot pans, or marble or Corian inserts as pastry slabs.

OTHER ACCESSORIES

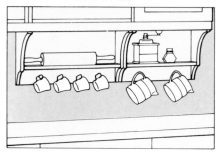

MID-RANGE CUPBOARDS
Style Designed to fit in the wall space between base units and wall units.
In use Can be open shelves or have sliding doors – very useful for small jars, bottles and items which would get lost in a large cupboard.

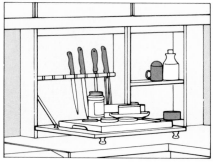

MID-RANGE CHOPPING BOARDS
Style A chopping board which folds away when not in use with a special rack behind for storing knives and cooking implements.
In use Handy – as these larger chopping boards are usually heavy and awkward to store.

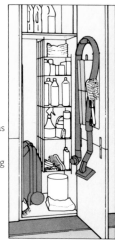

TALL UNIT FITTINGS
Style Some of the most useful extras you can buy for a tall unit are purpose-made, plastic-coated wire brackets or hooks for storing ironing boards, vacuum cleaners and accessories, saucepan lids, etc.
In use Most of these are readily available from sources other than the kitchen unit manufacturer, such as hardware and cookware shops.

EXTRAS FOR WALL UNITS

OPEN SHELVES
Style Rounded shelves which are wall-hung and finish off runs of wall units.

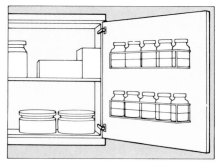

SPICE RACKS
Style Fitted to the inside of cupboard doors.
In use An easy-to-see way of storing small bottles and containers.

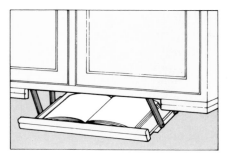

BOOKREST
Style A drop-down bookrest which, when closed, looks like part of the pelmet below a wall unit.
In use Somewhere to place open cookery books at eye-level – away from sticky worksurfaces.

Cookers, Ovens and Grills

Buying a cooking appliance is not just a case of buying what fits, or looks best or costs the least. Fuel options and personal requirements are just a few of the points to consider before choosing an appliance that should last for many, many years.

The choice of fuel is probably your first consideration, followed by the style of cooker you would like to have. You can choose between conventional freestanding cookers; slot-in cookers; built-in/built-under ovens with a separate hob or maybe one of the new worktop mini-cookers or a microwave oven.

Think, too, about how much and what kind of cooking you do. A built-in half size oven and microwave with a separate hob may suit you better than a more conventional cooker with a full-size oven. The checkpoints below will help you decide.

Depending on where you live, electricity, gas and solid fuel are the three main fuel options available.

FUELS

Electricity is universally available and considered by many to be the fuel of the future with rarely any supply problems; but it can be expensive, hence the popularity of more economical appliances such as microwaves. Recent developments include halogen and magnetic induction heating methods.
Gas is a relatively inexpensive source of energy, usually more responsive than electricity. The majority of homes have a natural mains gas supply but homes in rural areas without mains gas have the liquid petroleum alternative, also known as lpg. Piped in from bottles, cylinders or tanks stored outside, lpg relies on regular deliveries for convenience.
Solid fuel is not usually considered a cooking option unless as part of a space or water heating system. Agas and Rayburns burn coal but there are also wood-burning alternatives – suitable only in country areas with adequate wood storage and ash disposal facilities and no clean air restrictions as regards fuel.

CHECKPOINTS

When choosing which type of cooker to buy bear in mind the following points:
☐ Changing from gas to electric or the other way around means installation expenses.
☐ Is your kitchen large enough for a separate oven and hob or would a conventional or slide-in cooker save space?
☐ Do you do enough cooking to justify a full-sized oven. Would a microwave cooker be sufficient?

When choosing an oven bear in mind:
☐ Shelves should be supported and not tip, when partly pulled out.
☐ Glass doors enable food to be seen while cooking.
☐ Hinged doors should be reversible, able to be hung from either side.
☐ Drop down doors should be strong enough to support food and slope slightly towards the oven to prevent food slipping off.
☐ Removable doors and linings are easy to clean.
☐ Catalytic oven linings vaporize food splashes at medium to high temperatures leaving oven only needing a wipe over.
☐ Pyrolytic oven linings remove food splashes completely at very high temperatures but are more expensive and not very common.
☐ An interior oven light helps judge cooking through glass doors without opening them.
☐ Check controls are easy to reach, easy to turn on and are clearly marked.
☐ If the grill is inside the oven you won't be able to use them both at once.

COOKERS AND OVENS

FREESTANDING COOKERS

Style Traditionally, these consist of a single oven, combined with a hob and a grill which can either be at eye-level above the hob or waist-level just above the oven.
In use They are either gas or electric. Electric cookers need a 30 amp connection to the main fuse box and a heavy duty cable. Gas cookers are connected to the gas supply using a flexible hose which can be turned off and disconnected. Models with two roller feet can be moved easily; the other two feet should be adjustable to enable the cooker to be sited perfectly level.
Watchpoints Freestanding cookers are the most difficult to fit neatly into a run of fitted units. Check whether the insulation is good enough to place next to a fridge or food cupboard.

SLOT-IN COOKERS

Style Sleek and uncluttered, they are designed to slide between kitchen units to create a flush look or even to fit across corners. Improved insulation allows them to touch adjacent units and be sited next to fridges. Some models have a fold-down hob cover.
In use They can be gas or electric and many slot-ins now have dual fuel options, with gas hob and electric fan oven being the most popular combination, although halogen hobs are available on some. The grill can be separate at waist height or in the oven.
Watchpoints Look for adjustable feet to align with adjacent units. Check for a flame cut-off device when the hob is lowered if it is gas, or an indicator light showing the hob is still hot for electric.

BUILT-IN/BUILT-UNDER OVENS

Style Also known as split level cookers as the hobs are installed separately. They have a streamlined appearance and can be a single oven with or without integral grill, double oven or oven and microwave. The latest innovations usually appear on built-in appliances first.

In use Can be installed at a height or in a position which suits you best, making it ideal for people with back problems or to keep the oven out of reach of children. Allows you to have a combination of fuels – a gas hob and electric oven – and also to choose between different manufacturers.

Watchpoints Cost is the main disadvantage as they need a supporting housing unit and when the time comes to move house, they may be difficult to take with you or have only second-hand value to the new owner.

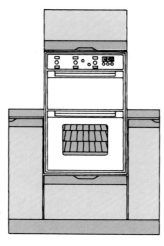

SOLID FUEL COOKERS

Style The cooker incorporates the fuel burning unit and is therefore quite large. Two or four oven models are available, the latter suitable for very large families or guest houses. Both have a boiling plate and simmering plate covered by insulating lids which can take up to three pans each. Available in a range of colours.

In use Coal or wood is traditionally used but oil, gas or electric models are available. Best used in conjunction with space and water heating requirements. Can be allied to a boiler to run a central heating system.

Watchpoints In general, temperatures on solid fuel appliances are hard to regulate accurately and there is no grilling facility; fuel supplies can be erratic especially in bad weather.

COOKING METHODS

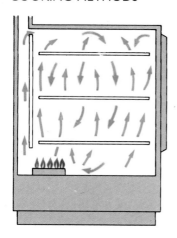
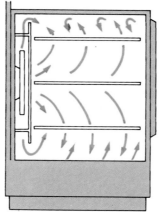
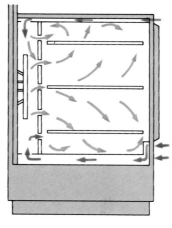
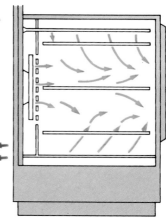

NATURAL CONVECTION

The traditional heat pattern with the top shelf being the hottest, the bottom the coolest. Found on most gas ovens and still a few electric models. Has a slightly drying effect when cooking – an advantage for some foods. For traditional cooks and those who do not need to batch bake.

FAN-ASSISTED/DUCTED FORCED CONVECTION

Use various methods to keep temperatures even throughout the oven. Fan-assisted ovens (above) circulate air round the oven, ducted fans (right) send heated air through ducts at shelf levels. Do not need pre-heating therefore economical, especially if you can fill each shelf, and lower cooking temperatures mean fewer splashes. Food keeps moist and shrinks less. Some of the most sophisticated models have a temperature probe for accurate roasting. The hum or vibration from the fan can be annoying. Mostly found on electric ovens but sometimes available on gas.

MULTI-FUNCTION OVENS

Give a wide range of functions – natural convection, fan-assisted, bottom heat only, top heat only, defrost and automatic roast (sealing at a high temperature before temperature automatically lowers) are the most commonly available. Most frequently found on electric built-in ovens.

GRILLS

The position of the grill depends on the type of cooker – eye-level grills are only available on conventional cookers or inside a built-in oven. Otherwise the grill is at waist level, either in a separate compartment above the oven or inside the oven itself. A grill set inside the oven means you cannot grill and roast at the same time – if this is likely to be a problem consider buying a table top grill.

Make sure the grill pan handles are secure and that it is large enough for your needs. A reversible grill rack and two shelf positions make a separate grill more versatile.

GAS

Gas grills either have a series of jets along the back or along two sides, or the flames work out from a central plate. Gas grills can be adjusted by lowering the jets.

ELECTRIC

Electric grills have a single or double element – the former for small portions.
Rotisserie and kebab attachments are available for some grills but do not buy them unless you are sure you will make full use of them.

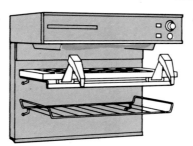

gas grill

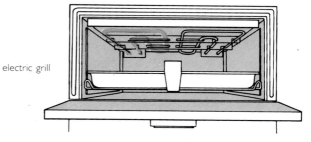

electric grill

Hobs, Microwaves and Small Ovens

HOBS

Either gas or electric, part of a conventional cooker or separately built in. If there is a hob cover it should cut out power to the rings if inadvertently lowered. Most built-in hobs are for the right-handed, if you are left-handed, look for reversible controls.

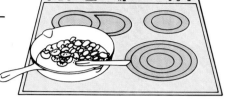

ELECTRIC RADIANT RING

Style Usually found on freestanding cookers and a few built-in hobs.

In use Modern rings respond faster than earlier models. Look for dual circuit rings where the inner ring only can be switched on for economy when using small pans.

Watchpoints Built-in radiant hobs are deep so you may lose drawer space underneath. Tops may be awkward to clean even though they hinge or the spill tray slides out.

ELECTRIC SEALED/SOLID HOTPLATES

Style The electric element is covered by a thin metal sheet.

In use Easier to clean and less space consuming than radiant versions. Look for a range of hotplate sizes and ratings with simmerstats or pan savers which keep foods at a steady simmer or prevent liquids boiling over. May also be available as large rectangular shapes for fish kettles.

Watchpoints Not as responsive as radiant rings.

ELECTRIC CERAMIC

Style Attractive streamlined appearance which can double as an extra worktop when cool (but do not use as a cutting surface).

In use Some ceramic hobs have dual circuit control for economy when using small pans.

Watchpoints Should have residual heat indicators as a safety feature. You may need a new set of pans for maximum contact on the very flat surface. Standard ceramic hobs not as fast as radiant or sealed ones.

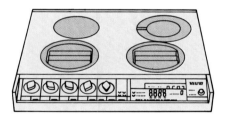

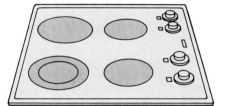

HALOGEN CERAMIC

Style A recent invention. Some models have four cooking zones, others five and one or two may combine two halogen zones with two conventional electric ceramic areas.

In use The tungsten halogen filament produces an instant heat when turned on and the range of temperatures can be controlled very precisely. The cooking area glows red when on.

Watchpoints Not widely available and very expensive at the present time.

MAGNETIC INDUCTION CERAMIC

Style The electric hob of the future, it uses a coil under a ceramic surface.

In use The coil generates magnetic energy only when a ferrous pan is in place; the pan and its contents get hot while the hob surface remains cool.

Watchpoints Not widely available and very expensive at the moment. You may have to replace your existing cooking pans.

GAS CERAMIC

Style A few manufacturers produce hobs with gas burners set under a ceramic surface.

In use Are as easy to clean as electric ceramic hobs and the top can double as a work surface.

Watchpoints They are expensive to buy and do not have the speed and controllability of an ordinary gas burner.

DUAL FUEL

Style Usually two gas burners and two sealed electric rings on the same hob. May also come as three gas/one electric combination.

In use Ideal if you want to combine the features of both fuels.

Watchpoint They usually cost more than the single fuel equivalent.

GAS BURNERS

Style The gas burners are set in a recessed tray covered by stainless steel or enamelled pan supports. The supports usually lift off in two or four parts for cleaning. All four burners may be the same size or there may be two large and two small, the latter for cooking at a low heat. Most modern cookers have spark ignition to light the burners which is electrically or battery operated.

Many slot-in cookers and built-in hobs have fold down lids, the safest being counterbalanced with automatic gas cut-out if the lid is lowered with the burners still on. The lid can be a useful resting place for pots and pans when cooker is not in use.

In use The gas burners can be adjusted simply and quickly. Some hobs have thermostatically controlled burners which adjust the flame to maintain a previously set heat.

Watchpoint Look for a slim divider between controls and burners on built-in hobs to protect controls from excessive heat. An automatic re-ignition device which relights a burner which has gone out is a useful safety feature. Check the pan supports are able to carry very small pans.

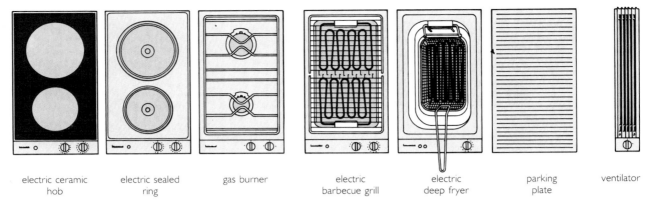

electric ceramic hob   electric sealed ring   gas burner   electric barbecue grill   electric deep fryer   parking plate   ventilator

MODULAR GAS OR ELECTRIC

Style Also called domino hobs, these are half width hobs which can be installed in any combination. The choice includes electric ceramic, sealed ring, grill and deep fat fryer and gas burners. A parking plate to rest pans is a useful addition.

In use Ideal for a very small kitchen or for the cook who has very specific needs. A surface mounted ventilator grille is also available.

Watchpoint More expensive than conventional hobs.

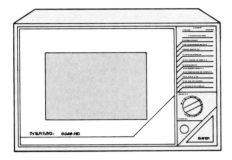

△ The basic microwave has manual settings with or without a rotating turntable.

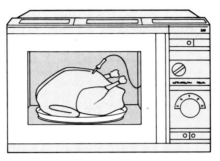

△ A rotating antenna in floor or ceiling and temperature probe adds versatility.

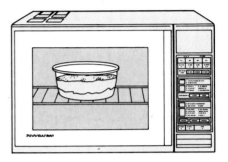

△ Electronic settings and an internal shelf feature on some expensive models.

MICROWAVE COOKERS

Microwaves can be used to defrost, cook and reheat food. Capacity is limited so unless cooking for one or two they must be used in conjunction with conventional oven and hob.

They work using a magnetron that produces waves which vibrate the water molecules in the food; this causes friction and heat which does the cooking. The process is fast and the oven needs no warm-up period so it is energy saving and economical. The short cooking time means that vitamins and minerals are retained in the food.

Porcelain, ceramic, glass, plastic, cardboard and paper containers can be used safely and washing up is reduced as food can be cooked and served in the same dish. Never use metal or foil containers or china which has a gold or silver trim as this damages the magnetron.

Most ovens are worktop models but some can be wall-mounted or built in.

Controls The simplest and cheapest ovens have a manual timer setting up to about 30 minutes with two power levels – a low one for defrosting and slow cooking and a high one for reheating and fast cooking. More expensive and sophisticated models have electronic controls with timers which can be set up to 2 hours, programming facilities which enable pre-setting of a series of operations such as defrost, followed by cooking and finally keeping warm. These models also have a choice of power levels.

A temperature probe attached inside the oven and inserted into the centre of the food can be set to a particular temperature and gives a far more accurate method of cooking. When the food reaches the set heat the microwave switches to keeping the food warm.

Interior layout Food must be turned at least once in the oven during the process to ensure even cooking. This is done by hand on the cheapest models; medium priced models have a rotating turntable which turns during cooking but this can restrict the space in an oven or the shape of dish you can use. More expensive ovens have a rotating antenna beneath or above the floor or ceiling which gives an even distribution of microwaves. They may also have a shelf which is useful for stacking several shallow dishes in the oven at one time.

Combination oven A microwave oven on its own cannot boil eggs, deep fry, cook pastry or Yorkshire pudding. It is not successful for large roasts or a large number of baked potatoes, and food can look pale and bland even when cooked. To overcome this, ovens which combine microwave, grilling and convection methods of cooking have been developed. This means a choice between microwave, grilling or convection cooking or any combination of microwave/convection grill.

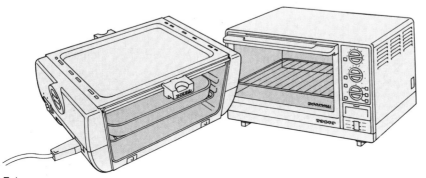

WORKTOP COOKERS

There are many small table top electric cookers available. They do not replace a conventional oven but are a useful addition. Most cook using the convection method with an internal grill for browning or grilling. Some have a steaming facility which is particularly good for fish or vegetables, while others include a removable hotplate on top.

Fridges
and Freezers

FRIDGES

There are a variety of types and sizes available, but one of the first decisions to make before you buy a fridge is where it is going to be situated in your kitchen.

Size Most fridges are freestanding and range in size from small models, which sit on a work surface, to those which stand at work-surface height (about 80-90cm) and the tallest types which are twice this height. Capacities range from 50 litres (tabletop) to about 150 litres (standard work-surface height) and around 280 litres for the largest.

Worktop-high fridges come with laminated tops which can be used as work surfaces. Alternatively they can be slotted under a kitchen worktop to fit in with a row of units. If you prefer a fridge to be an integral part of a fitted kitchen you can choose between buying a coloured fridge (some manufacturers offer a wide choice of colours) or a fridge which has a special framework for attaching kitchen unit doors.

Frozen food compartments The inside of a fridge is always at a temperature of between 4 – 7° C. Most models also have a frozen food compartment which is usually suitable only for storing pre-frozen food. You should not freeze fresh food, unless the compartment has a four-star rating. Fridges without a frozen food compartment are known as larder fridges (these are frost-free and defrost automatically). They are ideal if you already have a freezer.

Star ratings Frozen food compartments should carry star ratings to indicate how they must be used. One star indicates frozen food can be stored for up to one week; two stars, up to one month and three stars, up to three months. Four stars indicate that food can be frozen from fresh.

Mechanism Most fridges (and all freezers) are run by compressors (basically speaking a compressor is a motor-driven pump which cools and pumps a coolant around the fridge). This produces the intermittent hum that fridges often make. A small number of fridges have no compressor and work by means of an electric element or gas jet. They make no noise, but are more expensive to buy and run.

Leaving room All fridges and freezers require adequate air circulation, so when slotting a fridge into a run of kitchen units, make sure that you leave about 10cm of space above and at the back. Some models have a cage or grill which protects the workings at the back so you don't have to leave any space around these models.

FEATURES CHECKLIST

Before buying a fridge consider which features you require:
- ☐ Salad bin/drawers
- ☐ Dairy shelf
- ☐ Frozen food compartment
- ☐ Interior light
- ☐ Drinks dispenser
- ☐ Ice maker
- ☐ Left/right interchangable door hang
- ☐ Adjustable feet (to alter height of fridge)
- ☐ Egg storage
- ☐ Automatic defrost
- ☐ Shelf flaps for standing bottles
- ☐ Warning lights

TYPES OF FRIDGE

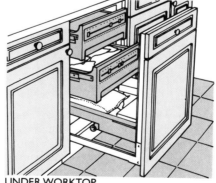

UNDER WORKTOP
Style A fridge which stands at worktop-level is generally between 80-90cm high with an approximate capacity of 150 litres and a width of 55cm. The conventional style has a left or right opening door, but the latest innovation

(above left) pulls out like a drawer.
In use This fridge, as well as fitting below the work-surface, also fits above it, so it can be built into a tall kitchen unit.

FREESTANDING CABINET
Style This model is much taller than a worktop, (almost twice the height at around 100-140cm). It can have a capacity of about 200-280 litres.
In use This fridge is most suitable for large families or people who use a fridge a lot. Choose between models with or without a freezer compartment. A fridge like this is generally very versatile as it has adjustable shelves and storage compartments.

TABLETOP
Style This is the smallest fridge that you can buy (around 55-litre capacity). It is designed to sit on the work surface or can even sit on the top of a worktop-level freezer.
In use Ideal for single people living on their own or for use in tents and caravans when space is at a premium.

FREEZERS

Preserving food by freezing is relatively quick, simple and effective. Freeze home-made food, fresh food or simply store pre-frozen goods so you are prepared for unexpected visitors, unplanned meals or meals which you can knock up in a minute.

Safe temperature The food is packed and frozen at a temperature of −18° C or even below. This provides a safe environment where bacteria cannot multiply. The storage period varies depending on the particular food, but commercially frozen food can be stored for up to three months and your own fresh/home cooked food for much longer.

Size Size and dimensions are up to you and your needs, but freezers generally range from the tabletop size (55 litre capacity) to worktop height upright models (around 100 litres), taller uprights (up to 200 litres) to the largest chest freezer (500 litres).

Features For those who pre-freeze food in their freezer (rather than loading it with pre-frozen foods), a fast-freeze facility on a freezer overrides the thermostat to ensure that the temperature is sufficiently low to freeze fresh food without affecting the load already frozen.

For a list of the types of features available on modern freezers see our checklist.

DEFROSTING

Fridges Some need to be defrosted manually by disconnecting the power and allowing the frost which forms in the fridge, to thaw. Others defrost automatically — they are referred to as frost-free and defrost on a day-to-day basis, so there is never any build-up of frost. Semi-automatic defrosting types are press-button operated.

Freezers Although you can buy frost-free freezers too, many still defrost manually. But life is made easier for the freezer owner by a draining spout at the base of a freezer. When the freezer has defrosted, the water runs out through the spout so all that is required is a bucket under the spout to catch the water. In other models water collects in a removable tray in the base.

FREEZER FEATURES CHECKLIST
- ☐ Adjustable feet
- ☐ Lock
- ☐ Interior light
- ☐ Interchangeable door hang
- ☐ Automatic defrost
- ☐ Defrost spout
- ☐ Baskets
- ☐ Separate drawer compartments
- ☐ Freezer drawer for soft fruits
- ☐ Fast freeze facility

TYPES OF FREEZER

CHEST

Style This has a top-opening lid. Originally a chest freezer was a long rectangular shape but squat, box-shaped freezers with top-opening lids are now available. Sizes range in capacity from about 100 litres up to 500 litres or more.

In use Frozen food is usually organized inside the chest in removable wire baskets or trays, which makes packing and retrieving food easier than simply piling it in.

Watchpoint The nature of the rectangular-shaped chest freezer means that it takes up a relatively large area of floor space in your kitchen and many chest freezers are kept in an out-house, utility room or even the garage. Most models are lockable to make them secure.

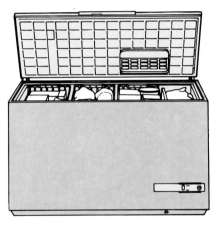

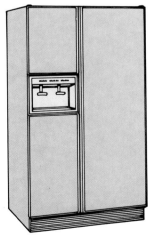

UPRIGHT

Style This has a front opening door and comes in a variety of heights ranging from tabletop size to worktop-height and above.

In use Takes up less floor space than the chest freezer and also can be integrated into a fitted kitchen, as most are available with frames to which cupboard door fascias can be attached to match kitchen units. Food is usually organized in pull-out drawers or baskets.

FRIDGE-FREEZER

Style This is a fridge and an upright freezer in one. Choose from a model which has a larger fridge and smaller freezer, a larger freezer and smaller fridge or divided exactly in half. Also choose whether you want a fridge on top or below.

In use Some fridge-freezers run off one compressor, others off two. Those with one means that in the event of a mechanical breakdown both fridge and freezer compartments fail.

FRIDGE-FREEZER CENTRES

Style Big American-style models usually have two opening doors (they are like two upright models next to each other) and apart from being much larger than standard fridge-freezers, are more expensive.

In use These often contain ice-making machines and cold drink dispensers. Ice or drink is dispensed through an opening on the outside of the door, which means you don't have to open the door every time you want to use this facility.

Kitchen Sinks

MATERIALS

Stainless steel is still the most popular choice for a kitchen sink. It's tough, hardwearing, lightweight and well-priced with many designs at the budget-end of the price range. It can be pressed into almost any space and easily hole-punched to take a range of taps and accessories. A drawback with stainless steel sinks is the clatter of china and cutlery on it, so make sure you choose a sink with a vibration damper underneath – just look for a black pad stuck to the underneath of the sink. Your sink should also be earthed to prevent the risk of getting an electric shock. Although you can do this yourself, it is advisable to contact a qualified electrician to do the work for you.

Vitreous enamel can have a matt or a gloss finish which is baked on to cast iron, or more often these days on to pressed steel. These sinks used to have a bad reputation for chipping easily, but these days manufacturers are successfully overcoming this problem by applying a much thinner coat of enamel to make it more chip-resistant. The edges of the sink are still the most vulnerable point, though, so treat them with care. Enamelled sinks are heat- and stain-resistant, but you should clean them with a non-abrasive liquid or cream household cleaner to avoid scratches.

Ceramic or fireclay sinks are available in modern shapes, sizes and colours. New ones are scratchproof and almost non-chip; they're virtually stain-resistant too. (These properties are all improvements on the older types, which were prone to scratching, crazing and chipping.)

Brass has a tendency to scratch and it must be cleaned with a proper brass cleaner followed by a regular polish with a brass product. Available as a sink/drainer unit or separate components, including taps.

Corian is a cast, man-made stone that looks and feels like marble, though it is far tougher, stain- and heat-resistant. The sinks come in different sizes and can be permanently bonded to a matching continuous work surface. Any tiny scratches can easily be erased with an abrasive cleaner or very fine sandpaper. Corian is very expensive but virtually indestructible.

Asterite is a tough blend of silica and resin, with the colour running right through the material. It has a very high resistance to heat, stains and scratches and is also easy to clean.

Polycarbonate is another man-made material that is available in a number of manufacturers' ranges. It can cope with temperatures up to 150°C and has some noise-absorbing qualities as well.

Fradura is a moulded rock-like composite material made up from glass and minerals, chemically bonded with resin. Impact and stain-resistant, it withstands temperatures up to 200°C.

SIZES

Decide if you want a sit-on sink which literally sits on top of a base unit, or an inset sink. Inset sinks sit in a hole cut in the work surface and offer the widest choice of shapes and sizes.

Also consider what size you want the bowl to be and the combination of bowl/drainer. Choose from single sink and drainer, double sink and drainer, sink and double drainer and so on.

Where space is limited, a combination of one-and-a-half bowls plus a drainer offers practical use of space. A half-bowl usually measures about half (or even a quarter) of the size of a standard sink – ideal for fitting a waste disposer. Always go for the largest possible sink to fit the available space.

What looks like an extremely shallow bowl (30–70mm deep) is best employed as a drainer – although it comes in handy for washing or straining vegetables, as it has its own waste.

When space is really tight, separate sinks and drainers are the most versatile as you can put them as close or as far apart as you like.

You could, of course, go without a drainer. Many modern sinks come with draining racks which fit into them to hold clean crockery, pots and pans. (See 'Optional extras' over page).

Bowl sizes vary enormously from the smallest round bowls – 380mm in diameter – to a big, rectangular bowl 450mm wide. Most bowls should measure at least 160–180mm deep to be practical for washing up.

Check that the largest item you need to wash on a regular basis, fits into it. Some sinks come with pre-made holes for taps and accessories, others give you the option to have the holes punched out where you require them. (Most tap holes are 35mm in diameter).

Standard wastes are 38mm in diameter or a larger 89mm for a strainer waste – this incorporates a removable strainer which catches scraps of food etc. Decide at this stage whether you want a waste disposer – most fit the 89mm waste which is the most practical size, although you can now get adaptors that enable disposers to be fitted to smaller wastes, although these are more restricting in use.

All sinks are made to fit worktops of between 27–47mm thick.

STYLES OF SINK

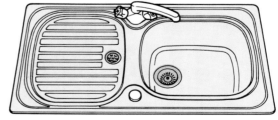

STANDARD
Style Conventionally made from polished stainless steel (but also available in enamelled steel and ceramic). It is designed to sit over a kitchen sink unit.
In use Usually incorporates a stainless steel upstand, which acts as a splashback and has a lip along the front edge to finish off the sink unit. A single sink/drainer unit is about 1000mm × 500mm, but there are variations such as a sink and double drainer (as shown).

INSET RECTANGULAR
Style 'Inset' means that it is designed to drop into a hole cut into a worktop. Therefore it doesn't come right to the edge of your worktop – probably ideally positioned 50–60mm in from the edge.
In use This sink can be made from stainless steel and is widely available in enamelled steel, ceramic and a variety of man-made plastic-related materials in a range of colours. Bowl sizes vary so make sure you choose one big enough.

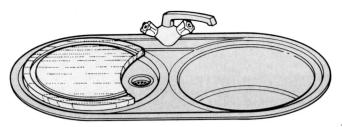

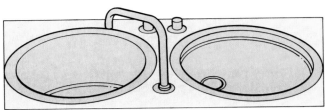

INSET CIRCULAR
Style A variation on the rectangular shape.
In use The deep bowl is for washing up, the shallow bowl is ideal for washing vegetables but is intended

as a drainer. It could be fitted with a waste disposal unit so peelings and the like can be pushed straight down the waste. A wooden cover-cum-chopping board for the drainer is often an optional extra.

SEPARATE CIRCULAR UNITS
Style Separate bowl and drainer – fit snugly into corners of worktops.
In use particularly good where space is limited as they are available in small sizes (450mm in diameter – although there are bigger ones on

offer). Choose from stainless steel or enamelled steel versions. A draining basket is available to sit in the bowl and a teak chopping board-cum-cover fit neatly over the drainer.

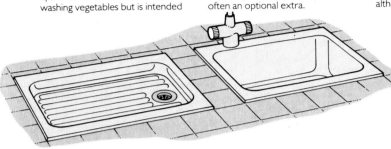

SEPARATE SQUARE UNITS
Style Inset square bowl and drainer made as separate units.
In use These are designed to give maximum flexibility, so if necessary they can be inset into worktops at opposite ends of your kitchen.

Each unit measures about 500mm × 500mm. The drainer is available with a half-bowl incorporated. These are made in stainless steel, enamelled steel and most other materials, including ceramic.

TRIANGULAR
Style Triangular-shaped bowl and drainer set into a rectangular normal-sized sink unit. Also available with a compact half-bowl, built in.
In use Bowl and drainer set at an angle to each other. This looks

attractive and many people also find the positioning of the washing-up bowl very comfortable in use. Available in stainless steel, enamelled steel, or man-made plastic-related materials.

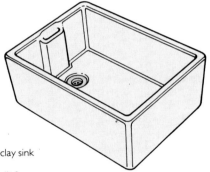

BUTLER STYLE
Style The old-fashioned fireclay sink is having a revival!
In use This sink is not only built for washing-up but is roomy and sturdy enough for hand-washing in. Sizes range from 455 × 380 × 205mm deep to

915 × 610 × 305mm deep. There is also a fireclay drainer to match.
Watchpoint You will probably only find this available in white.

CORNER
Style A sink that cuts corners! Designed to fit into corners which might normally be wasted space.
In use This inset sink sits diagonally across a corner area. The large basin

is for washing-up, the other two for rinsing and drying. Available in a variety of materials.
Watchpoint Mixer tap should swivel and also be long enough to reach over the smaller bowls for rinsing.

OPTIONAL EXTRAS

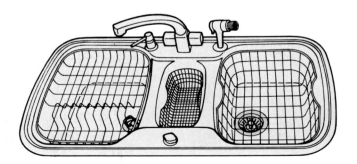

PERFORATED DRAINER
Made in plastic, this thick perforated tray fits over the bowl. Useful for draining and straining. Although the flat variety (shown) is most useful, some manufacturers offer perforated bowls which sit in the sink bowl itself.

DRAINER
Plastic-coated wire basket – often incorporating a plate drainer – sits over the top of a bowl so that once the dishes have been washed they can drain over it.
This is ideal for those who only have a bowl and no drainer.

BASKET
This is also made from plastic-coated wire. It sits inside the main bowl to protect your crockery from chipping or cracking while washing up.

CHOPPING BOARD/COVER
Wooden cover (usually made from teak wood) to put over the main bowl when not in use. It doubles up as a chopping board, so is ideal in small kitchens as it means when the sink is not being used, you can use it as a food preparation surface.

Choosing Kitchen Taps

MATERIALS

The look and the feel of your kitchen taps is mainly governed by the material they are made from.

Brass This is the base metal for most taps. However, solid brass or brass-plated taps are the perfect foil for period-style kitchen units. They can be polished with a high shine or be given an antiqued finish.

Chrome Generally the cheapest type of material from which taps are made. Chromium plate suits all styles of sinks and kitchens and is usually offered on nearly all tap designs.

Porcelain Not used for modern taps, although porcelain decoration on period-style taps is experiencing something of a revival at the moment – mostly teamed up with brass.

Nylon Highly-coloured nylon taps are a good way to brighten up a plain sink or kitchen. Very hardwearing, they stay cool even when you're running the hot water through them. They're easy to clean too.

Enamel Some of the brightest coloured taps have an enamel finish, baked on to a metal base to give a tough finish.

HOW A TAP WORKS

In a conventional type of tap the valve and washer are the parts which operate the flow of water. But on the most modern type of tap the valve and washer are replaced by a ceramic disc or cartridge. These are claimed to work more efficiently as the disc is supposed to be virtually immune to wear and tear or corrosion from water and limescale build-up. This should reduce the chance of leaks and drips and should therefore last longer.

Valves and washers are still found on many taps which you buy today, though; the newest types are coated with a non-stick finish to stop hardwater deposits forming on them.

RULES AND REGULATIONS

Whichever type of tap you choose, it should conform to the British Standard BS5412/3 part 1 and 2, 1976. This means the tap has been tested to ensure that the rate at which water flows through the tap is adequate. (For pillar taps it is 9.5 litres per minute, and double that for mixer fittings.) Your taps should also satisfy any local water by-law which safeguards against the wastage and contamination of domestic water supplies.

Ask at your local library for the **Directory of Fittings and Materials** which gives details of all the by-law installation requirements.

MAKING A CHOICE

Decide on the sort of taps you want before buying a sink, then you can make sure you order one with the correct tap holes. Choose taps in keeping with your kitchen units, bearing in mind their style and colour. Also, look out for manufacturers who make co-ordinating sinks and taps in matching colours and finishes.

Styles There are two basic choices in tap design: pillars or mixers.

Pillars are the more conventional style of tap. You require two of these – one for hot and one for cold water. More often than not a pillar tap is mounted on the sink itself. However, the older-style wall-mounted taps are still available; these are suitable for use with a butler sink (see below) or anywhere when mounting taps on the sink is not possible.

Mixers mix hot and cold water through one spout. A dual-flow mixer tap appears to mix both hot and cold water, but in fact each supply runs along its own separate channel in the spout. A true mixer really does mix hot and cold together, but must be installed by a plumber so both water supplies are of equal pressure. There are mixer taps which are installed through a single taphole in the sink unit – these are called monobloc mixers. And there are mixers which have to be installed through two tapholes. These are called two-piece or deck-mounted mixers.

When buying kitchen mixers, remember to look out for those which have swivel spouts (strictly speaking a fixed spout is really only suitable for a bathroom washbasin). Also, if you have a sink unit which has more than one bowl (such as one and a half bowls plus a drainer), make sure that the spout is long or high enough for you to direct water into both bowls.

PILLAR TAPS

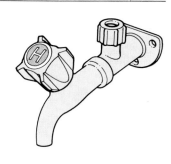

TRADITIONAL
Style Individual hot and cold water taps fit on to a horizontal surface.
In use The cross-head tap tends to make for a good grip: easy to turn off and on even with greasy hands.

MODERN
Style Fit on to horizontal surface. Usually have Perspex-encased heads.
In use Try the head for grip – often is is so chunky that it's tricky to turn with wet or greasy hands.

LEVER-OPERATED
Style A lever replaces the traditional tap head. Fitted with ceramic discs, a quarter-turn turns the water on and off again.
In use You need one tap for hot and one for cold water. Easy to control so very good for the elderly.

WALL-MOUNTED
Style Designed to be wall-mounted – often referred to as 'bib' taps.
In use Perfect accompaniments to the old-fashioned butler sink which is made of fireclay and has no surface upon which taps can easily be mounted.

MIXER TAPS

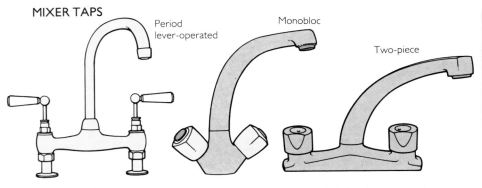

Period lever-operated

Monobloc

Two-piece

CONVENTIONAL

Style These taps are conventional in the sense that they have the 'conventional' workings – they all operate with a valve and washer. However, they vary widely in style from a brass, period-type, lever-operated mixer (which is two-piece so requires two tapholes) to the more modern-looking monobloc and two-piece mixers made from brightly-coloured enamel and shiny chromium plate with encased heads.

In use They all obviously combine hot and cold water in one spout – and have swivel spouts.

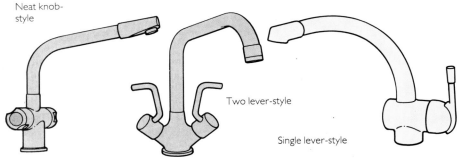

Neat knob-style

Two lever-style

Single lever-style

QUARTER-TURN

Style Monobloc mixers all fitted with ceramic discs – water comes on/off by a quarter turn.

In use Choose from a mixer with neat knobs (can be tricky to turn with greasy/wet hands), or a single lever that turns one way for hot and the other for cold water (lever can go either side of spout to suit right- or left-handers), or the mixer with long levers which can be operated by elbows.

Soap dispenser

Rinse-head

Spatula attachment

ACCESSORIES

A 'rinse head' is a brush connected to a flexible hose (hidden under the sinktop) which lifts out for use. When a lever is pressed it sends a spray of water on to the dirty dishes. This is handy if you have a sink which incorporates a bowl with a wire basket in it – once the dishes are washed they can be 'hosed down' while sitting in the basket. You can buy interchangeable heads for it such as a **spatula** to scrape pots and pans.

A **soap dispenser** holds liquid soap (washing-up liquid) under the sink in a reservoir. When the small 'tap' on top of the sink is pressed, it squirts soap into the washing-up bowl.

TAP HEADS

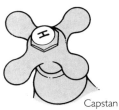

Capstan

Shrouded

Lever handle

There are three basic types of handle: the traditional **capstan head** with the cross top often called a cross head, the modern **shrouded or encased head** made from Perspex or metal or the **lever handle**.

The capstan head – the traditional design – has a centre screw that secures the head on to the rest of the tap. The shrouded head is a distinctive chunky style – the fixing screw is hidden under a cap on the top of the head. The lever handle tap has a lever to operate the tap. The same colour and material as the body of the tap, it works when it is pressed up/down or from side to side.

HOT WATER DISPENSERS

This is a tap with a difference. It is mounted on your sink top alongside your ordinary hot and cold taps and provides instant steaming hot water. A press of the lever draws up boiling water from a tank stored beneath the sink. It is a quick and economical alternative to boiling an electric kettle as it can be used to make tea, coffee, gravy, stocks etc, and costs less to operate than a 40 watt bulb.

Watchpoint The water really is boiling – so young children shouldn't have access to it.

CHECKLIST

☐ Do the taps and sink unit look right together?

☐ Are there enough tapholes in the sink to accommodate the taps you have chosen?

☐ Consider the height of taps – especially if the kitchen sink is to be used to fill buckets etc.

☐ Choose taps that fit in with the overall look of the kitchen – yellow plastic taps might not suit a traditional-style room.

☐ Taps must be hardwearing. Porcelain taps in the kitchen might not be as suitable as porcelain taps in the bathroom.

☐ If any type of hose – for the garden or for a washing machine – has to be fitted to the taps, make sure the taps are suitable.

☐ Think of cleaning – don't choose taps that need lots of cleaning if you are not keen on housework!

☐ If taps are for someone elderly, make sure they can use them.

☐ Some of the chunkier tap heads might look attractive, but try them out in the shop to see if they give you a good grip – even when your hands are wet or sticky.

Waste Disposers and Bins

The frightening thing about kitchen waste is the sheer volume which is created in the average home. A lot of this is due to modern packaging materials — particularly cardboard wrapping, plastic containers and metal cans — but a good part of your rubbish is likely to be left-over food, vegetable waste, or fish and meat bones, which tend to smell, attract flies and generally be a nuisance.

At one time, of course, rubbish disposal could be kept to a minimum: vegetable waste went on the compost heap, spare food was fed to the animals, anything combustible went into the stove and only metal things really needed to be thrown away. But these days things are different — not all households have a compost heap, so decaying matter has to be disposed of hygienically and all other rubbish put out for the dustman to collect.

A waste disposer fitted to the kitchen sink is an ideal way of getting rid of food scraps and waste. Usually electrically-operated, it fits underneath the sink waste outlet and converts rubbish into a fine slurry which is washed away down into the drains. There are two main types of electric waste disposer — batch-feed or continuous feed. With the batch feed type, you load up the waste disposer, put the cover/lid on and turn it to start it up. The continuous-feed type has a separate switch which you turn on to activate the disposer — waste material is then fed into it. (If you have children it is more advisable to go for the batch-feed disposer as this only works when the lid is in place.) With both types, cold water is left running into the sink during operation.

There is also a water-powered waste disposer. This has to be connected to the rising mains and the sheer force of water drives the cutting blades.

With all types of disposers it is advisable to get approval from your local authority before it is installed.

Most waste disposers are designed to fit the larger (89mm) size of waste outlet (fitted to some sinks with a basket strainer waste); some also have adaptors for fitting on to the more common 38mm waste outlet, but the restricted opening makes the disposer less easy to use.

Waste disposers can get jammed if fed with non-disposable waste. Some disposers have automatic reversing which will unjam obstructions, others have a manually-operated reversing switch or a release key (like a small wrench) for clearing jams.

A disposer needs its own 38mm waste pipe, fitted with a P-trap or an S-trap, leading to the main soil stack. Some have an additional connection to which a dishwasher drain hose can be attached which cuts down the number of waste pipes passing through the wall.

Bins In addition to a waste disposer you will also need a rubbish bin. This can either be freestanding or positioned inside a kitchen cupboard, either within the drawers or on the back of a door. Waste bins come in different materials (mainly plastic or metal) which are easy to keep clean, particularly if the bin can be fitted with an inner bin or a bin liner.

Compactor Where a lot of household rubbish is created, a compactor is useful. You simply feed rubbish into a large removable container inside a pull-down or pull-out drawer. When the unit is switched on, the rubbish is compressed to around a quarter of its volume. At the same time the compressed rubbish is packed into neat sacks which makes disposal easier. However, if you do intend to install a compactor, check with your local authority that the size and type of package that your machine produces can be handled by the authority's own compactors. A domestic compactor will usually fit neatly into a cupboard under a work surface.

WASTE DISPOSERS

CONTINUOUS-FEED DISPOSER
Style An unobtrusive electrically-powered device which fits beneath the kitchen sink.
In use The switch for a continuous-feed waste disposer is usually mounted on the wall or on the front of kitchen cupboards and once turned on, vegetable and food waste can be fed into the machine with the cold tap left running. Some models have a reversing switch to free light jams (some others are automatically reversing), to free major jams a small wrench or release key is usually supplied.
Watchpoint A perforated disc prevents cutlery accidentally falling into the machine when not in use and a rubber 'baffle' prevents water and waste from splashing out during use.

BATCH-FEED DISPOSER
Style Very similar in appearance to a continuous-feed machine, the batch-feed disposer fits under the kitchen sink too.
In use The on/off switch for this type of waste disposer is usually incorporated in the inlet neck. After a batch of waste has been put into the machine, the neck is rotated to turn the disposer on and rotated again to turn it off. A second load can then be added.
Watchpoint Generally more expensive than continuous-feed models, but because it only works with lid on, its major plus point is the safety aspect — important with young children about.

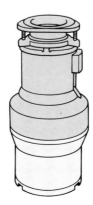

WATER-OPERATED DISPOSER
Style A plastic-bodied unit fitted to the sink waste outlet and also connected to the mains water supply.
In use No electrical connections are needed for this unit, which is operated by a simple control valve fitted into the sink surface. The pressure of water, which comes into it directly from the rising mains, drives the stainless steel cutting blades which pulp the waste. The unit is vibration-free and almost silent in use.
Watchpoint Permission needs to be obtained from local water authorities before connections are made to the rising main. Also, before buying this you must check that you have sufficient water flow and pressure to operate it. (Details are on the product's packaging).

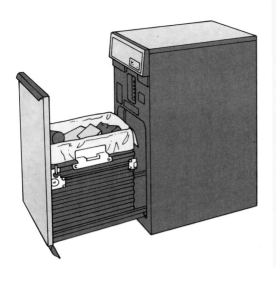

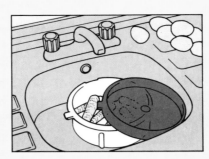

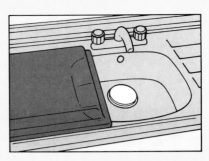

ACCESSORIES
There are a couple of accessories which fit on to a conventional electrically-motored disposer:
A vegetable peeler fits on to a shaft which goes down into the waste disposer. The vegetables are peeled within the covered bowl – peelings go straight into the waste disposer.
A laundry attachment also fits on to the shaft and acts as an agitator to wash lightly-soiled clothes in the sink. There is a cover/lid which fits standard rectangular sinks.

TRASH COMPACTORS
Style An electrically-operated machine which fits in place of a kitchen cupboard and can be fitted with a matching decor panel. It is usually about half the width of an automatic washing machine.

In use The pull-out drawer of the compactor is fitted with its own plastic or water-resistant paper sacks. After the rubbish has been put in, the machine applies a compressing force of about a ton which reduces the volume of the rubbish by 75 per cent.
Watchpoint To prevent young children operating the machine, it comes fitted with a removable safety key.

WASTE BINS

FREESTANDING KITCHEN BINS
Style Plastic or metal bins for the kitchen.
In use There are two main designs; flip-top or pedal. A flip-top (also called a swing bin) is generally 60-70cm high but is available in a smaller size; the hinged lid moves out of the way when rubbish is put in. On some models, the lid can be made to stay open.
    A pedal bin is usually smaller (around 45cm high). The lid lifts up when the pedal is pressed. Both types of bin can be fitted with bin liners; pedal bins usually have a second inner bin. Both styles of bin are available in a range of colours.

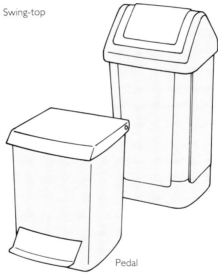

Swing-top

Pedal

Wall-mounted

WALL-MOUNTED BINS
Style A plastic bin which can be screwed to the wall. It has a lift-up lid.
In use Ideal as a smaller bin, this type needs one hand to open the bin while the other puts in the rubbish. It ranges in size from pedal-bin to flip-top bin size. Available in a range of colourways.

CONCEALED BINS

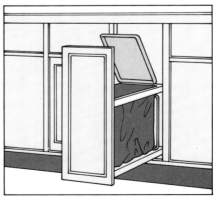

DOOR BACK STYLE
Style Waste bin fitted to the back of a kitchen unit door.
In use When you open the cupboard door the lid on the bin opens too. Usually situated under the sink – this makes good use of a limited amount of storage space. It also saves on floor space.

PULL-OUT STYLE
Style Fitted in a cupboard (mounted on the base of the unit) on its own pull-out sub-frame.
In use When the door opens the bin slides out. When you close the door the bin slides back into the cupboard on its frame and goes back into position under the lid (which does not move).

DRAWER STYLE
Style Bin is fitted in a deep drawer unit, which slides out when you pull out the drawer. The lid also pops up when bin is pulled out.
In use As with all the concealed bins, the inside of the drawer unit should be cleaned regularly to stop it smelling musty or mouldy.

Extractor Fans and Cooker Hoods

Cooking smells can permeate the whole house if they are not removed close to the source at the time they are produced. Opening a window or door may help, but in winter this means heat is lost.

If grease-laden air is not removed from kitchens, it will soon deposit itself on wall and ceiling surfaces.

Water vapour is one of today's greatest enemies – particularly now that many houses have been well draught-proofed, removing a lot of 'natural' ventilation. If the air inside the house contains too much moisture, this will condense on cold surfaces such as windows or walls which can lead to serious problems – rotten window frames, peeling wallpaper, black mould and crumbling plaster. Water vapour is most often created in kitchens and bathrooms – there are a number of steps which can be taken to reduce condensation, but one of the most effective is undoubtedly to remove water vapour at its source.

Ventilation is also needed in houses where solid fuel, gas, or oil-burning appliances are used with conventional chimneys.

The simplest way of providing a means for air to escape from kitchens is with a **window ventilator**. This fits into a circular hole in a window and is opened or closed by hand. The most popular ventilators have cord-operated shutters and rotor blades which are turned by the force of the air passing through them.

A more sophisticated type – the **trickle ventilator** – is fitted into the head of the window or the window frame. (Many double-glazed windows are supplied with these already built into the frames. A trickle ventilator is a vent which is open to the elements on the outside of the window but guarded with a cover on the inside – this can be opened and closed by hand as required.

The next step up is an electrically-operated ventilator – **an extractor fan**. This can be fitted in a circular hole cut either in a window or in an outside wall (with a grille on the outside wall). Alternatively it can be fitted in the ceiling, with a duct taking the air to the outside wall or, if upstairs (in the bathroom perhaps), to a vent outlet positioned in a roof tile.

The positioning of an extractor fan is important. It should be placed on the opposite side of the room to the main source of ventilation – usually an internal door leading into the room – and preferably with the source of water vapour/smells (cooker, sink, bath, or WC) in a line between the two.

Size is also important. A kitchen needs around 10 or more changes of air per hour when it is being used for cooking, so a kitchen measuring $3 \times 4m$ with a ceiling 2.3m high would need a fan capable of moving at least 276 cubic metres per hour.

Where an extractor fan is fitted in a room containing a WC which has only a small window (or no window at all), it is wired into the light switch so that it comes on automatically when the room is used and stays on for 15 minutes afterwards. Extracted air is then ducted out through an outside wall.

Some extractor fans can be fitted with humidity sensors so that they come on automatically when the humidity level in the room reaches a certain level – useful in bathrooms.

TYPES OF VENTILATOR

WINDOW VENTILATOR

Style A circular plastic non-electric device fitted in window panes. Pull cords open and close shutters. When open, air is let in to drive rotor blades round. When closed, the rotor blades remain fixed.
In use A ventilator needs a circular hole cut in a window pane (a job best left to a glazier) and provides only a slow rate of air change. Accessories include external stormguards, aperture reducers and fixing kits for mounting the ventilator in a wall.

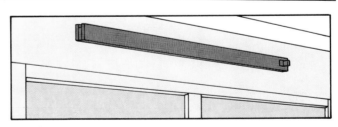

TRICKLE VENTILATOR

Style A two-part ventilator fitted over holes drilled through the head of the window or the window frames. Many aluminium double-glazed window units incorporate ventilators as a standard feature.
In use Usually adjustable by a lever, a trickle ventilator can be fitted when you do not want to cut a hole in the window pane. Especially suitable for use in living rooms.
Watchpoint Care is needed in drilling holes and any wood exposed should be primed or treated with wood preservative.

TYPES OF EXTRACTOR FANS

WINDOW MOUNTED

Style Circular, square, or rectangular electrically-operated fans fitted into a hole cut in the window.
In use An extractor fan needs to be connected to an electric supply and is operated either by a pullcord on the fan itself or by a separate electric switch on the wall. Most window fans have just one speed. All are fitted with shutters or louvres which prevent the wind blowing in when the fan is not operating. When in use, the fan makes about as much noise as a washing machine.
Watchpoint Cutting holes in double-glazed units and toughened glass panels is impossible, so the windows have to be specially ordered with the holes already cut. Even so, not all window-mounted fans are suitable for double-glazed windows, so check before you buy.

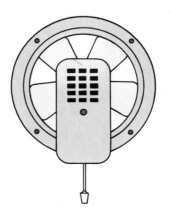

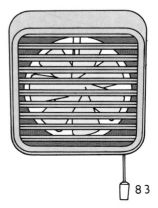

WALL-MOUNTED

Style A rectangular, electrically-operated fan mounted directly on an outside wall and connected to a duct.

In use Some wall-mounted extractor fans are similar if not identical to window-mounted versions – you just need different accessories to fit them. The fan is screwed to the inside wall and connected to a short length of ducting which connects in turn to an outlet grille on the outside wall. This if fitted with self-closing louvres. Some wall fans have two or three speeds for greater extraction rates and sometimes a reverse setting

which can be used in the summer for cooling the room.

Watchpoint Making the large round or rectangular hole necessary for a wall-mounted fan (and making good afterwards) is a job for a builder.

CEILING-MOUNTED

Style A neat and unobtrusive fan mounted in the ceiling above the source of smells or moisture.

In use The particular advantage of a ceiling-mounted extractor fan is that it can be installed directly over the point where it is needed – useful for a separate shower in a bathroom or bedroom. As well as ordinary extractor fans, there are ceiling-mounted fans which incorporate a light and are operated from the light switch.

Watchpoint Unless exhausting into a well-ventilated loft space , a ceiling-mounted extractor fan will need ducting to be fitted in the space

above the ceiling so it leads to an outlet grille in the outside wall or roof.

TYPES OF COOKER HOODS

A cooker hood is positioned over a cooker or separate hob to remove water vapour and cooking smells. There are two main types of cooker hood – ducted and recirculating.

Ducted cooker hood Air is taken through the hood's grease filter (usually made of latex foam, plastic or a similar material) and then it is extracted to the outside air via a lined hole in the wall and an outlet grille. The grease filter should be periodically washed. Generally a hood like this has two or three speeds. It is the more effective type of hood of the two.

Recirculating cooker hood Air is taken through a grease filter then through a charcoal filter, which removes smells and moisture. The 'purified' air is then returned to the room. In other words, the recirculating hood has no duct. As with a ducted cooker hood it usually has two or three speeds and needs an electrical supply. It has the advantage that it does not need to be fitted against an outside wall.

The performance of this type of cooker hood is drastically reduced if the filters are not cleaned and/or replaced regularly. Look for charcoal filters which are thick and densely packed for best results.

Sizes and positioning Most cooker hoods are designed to fit under cupboards above the cooker, so common sizes are 600mm, 900mm and 1000mm wide – which match up with kitchen cupboard widths. The height above the cooker or hob is important: the normal recommendation is between 600mm and 950mm above the hob, though instructions vary. If the cooker hood is positioned above a cooker with an eye-level grill, it should be at least 400mm above the top of the grill (for safety reasons). Most cooker hoods are fitted with lights which can be operated independently of the fan.

Hob downdraught extractor Where a separate hob is positioned in an island unit, or where several hob modules are sited next to one another, an alternative to a cooker hood is a downdraught extractor next to the hob itself and connected to a duct which takes the air to the outside via a hole in the wall.

CONVENTIONAL STYLE

Style These are wall-mounted and protrude beyond neighbouring cupboards about 15cm.

In use A pull-out visor extends the depth of the hood – this should be pulled out so that it extracts cooking fumes and steam from the front two hotplates on your hob or cooker.

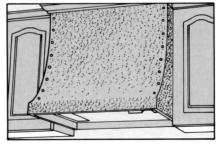

CANOPY STYLE

Style Popularly available in a beaten copper or brass to fit in with 'rustic-style' kitchens.

In use All the workings of the hood are hidden under the canopy. The canopy usually extends as high as the top of the adjacent kitchen units. Because of their size, they are very efficient.

INTEGRATED STYLE

Style Installed behind a hinged door or dummy front so they blend in with a fitted kitchen.

In use Operated by pulling the base of the door/front outwards so it protrudes over the hob. Usually automatically switches off again when the panel is pushed in.

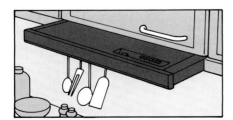

TELESCOPIC STYLE

Style Built into a wall unit, a slimline flat hood 50cm deep pulls out over the hob to trap steam and cooking smells.

In use When not in use this can be pushed back in to sit flush with adjacent wall cupboards. Available ducted or recirculating.

DOWNDRAUGHT EXTRACTOR

Style A slim, slotted powerful extractor fan installed next to the hob surface and sunk below worktop level, leaving only a metal grille exposed.

In use This type of extractor is usually fitted as part of the hob itself and is connected via ducting to the outside air in much the same way as an exhaust cooker hood.

Watchpoint Although neat and effective, this is very expensive. Because of its position, it does tend to get dirty from cooking spills or grease splashes. However, the grille can be removed for you to clean inside it with a damp cloth.

Choosing Dishwashers

A dishwasher can wash, rinse and dry a full load of lightly-soiled dishes in just 30 minutes. A normal wash will take up to 90 minutes – saving, on average, up to one hour of your own time each day. This time-saving adds up to more than two weeks over the course of a year.

SIZE

Most dishwashers are about the same size as a standard washing machine – about 85cm high by 60cm wide by 60cm deep. However, for homes where space is a problem, there are table-top models.

CAPACITY

Most standard dishwashers hold 12 international place settings. A setting consists of a dinner plate, soup plate, side plate, cup and saucer, glass, and a set of cutlery. However, one or two manufacturers make slightly larger machines which will take a load of up to 14 place settings.

Table-top models usually hold a load consisting of four to six place settings.

CONSTRUCTION

Most machines are front opening with a drop-down door. The inside is normally stainless steel and there are usually two racks – one upper and the other lower – on which to stand the dirty crockery. These sectionalized racks are made of plastic-coated wire and are generally mounted on nylon castors to allow them to slide in and out of the machine for ease of loading. There is a separate container for cutlery, which can sometimes be removed to make room for large pots and pans.

Much of a dishwasher's efficiency depends upon the shape and size of the racks and how easily the jetted water can get at the dirty plates.

DISHWASHING CYCLE

There are five basic steps in a normal washing programme when china, crockery and cutlery are cleaned and dried. These steps are:
☐ Cold water rinse.
☐ Heating – water from the cold supply is heated to about 60°C and thermostatically controlled.
☐ Washing – all dishwashers use water at high pressure to carry out their cleaning process. The water is distributed in the form of jets passing through rotating spray arms.
☐ Rinsing – the dishes are rinsed with hot, warm, or cold water.
☐ Drying – this is carried out either by a fan-assisted heater or by using the residual heat from the hot water after the rinsing cycle.

FEATURES

Some models have acoustic insulation to keep noise to a minimum during operation, which is important if you don't want to drown your guests' after-dinner conversation. Most models take rinse aid, which prevents spotting on glasses, and have built-in water softeners (usually coarse or granulated salt). These are useful in hard-water areas but the rinse aid and the water softener have to be recharged regularly.

Some more recently-designed dishwashers do not exceed a water temperature of 60°C – the heat at which scale forms – and these machines do not require a water-softening agent. However, there are machines which offer higher wash temperatures which may be needed for very dirty crockery.

Also to be found on some machines is an anti-flood facility which makes the machine safer to use at night.

PROGRAMMES

Most machines offer a variety of programmes to suit different wash loads. However, in practice you really only require a normal, light and intensive wash, plus a rinse-and-hold facility. The latter allows you to build up a full load during the day so that the day's washing-up can all be done at once.

Also useful are the plate-warming and half-load facilities on some makes.

SITING

Dishwashers can be freestanding or built in. In the case of the small models they can be put on a table top, draining board or worksurface. The worktop machines can be plumbed in or attached to kitchen taps but remember that you'll need space for pipes behind the washer, and room – at least 550mm clear space – to open the door.

INSTALLATION

Most machines are designed to be used with cold water – although many can be plumbed in to both hot and cold supplies. Pre-heated water may halve the time of the programme but it does use expensively-heated water on rinsing. Also, some food particles are best loosened with cold water – the first part of a normal programme – as hot tends to bake them on.

It is important to check that the water pressure at the point where the machine will be connected is sufficient – check with a service engineer before the machine is installed.

RUNNING COSTS

Many machines have energy-saving features. Electricity accounts for half the running costs, the rest being made up by detergent, water softener and rinse aid, so it makes sense to cut down on the programme times and temperatures of the wash where possible.

If your home uses night-time Economy 7 electricity, look for a machine which features a delay timer so that you can take advantage of the cheaper rate tariff. Most dishwashers are very economical to run; costing about £1.20 per week for the average family, compared with 50p if you wash up by hand.

ADVANTAGES

Time-saving is a major advantage and one of the main reasons for investing in a dishwasher. However, it is not the only plus point by any means.

Crockery washed in a dishwasher will literally sparkle when clean. A dishwasher will do wonders for every day

CONSIDERATIONS

It is not recommended to wash the following in your dishwasher:
☐ Crockery with gold, silver or platinum decoration
☐ Lead crystal or delicate glass should not be washed at high temperatures
☐ Bone, ivory or wooden handled cutlery
☐ Non-heatproof plastic
Plus you should not let stainless steel and silver come into contact with each other in the machine since they trigger off a chemical reaction.

glasses which will also come out gleaming. If properly loaded, a dishwasher rarely breaks anything and can be used for even your most precious china, provided that it does not have any gold or silver decoration. (See Considerations box on previous page.)

HYGIENE
A survey commissioned by the Electricity Council discovered that the bacteria count on handwashed and dried dishes was seven times higher than those washed and dried by machine. This is due to the fact that a machine uses much hotter water.

SAFETY
Most machines have a cut-out device which will turn off the power if the door is accidentally opened during operation. Some have childproof or retractable controls.

DISADVANTAGES
You may require extra crockery if you use the machine only once daily.

MAINTENANCE
Dishwashers require little maintenance, except such things as cleaning the special filters that trap dispersed food particles, refilling the rinse aid and keeping the salt topped up to soften water in hard-water areas. Some machines feature indicators to show when supplies are low. Choosing a well-designed machine with most of its parts accessible from the front will save you time and money.

CHECKLIST
Points to look for when choosing your dishwasher:
- ☐ Capacity
- ☐ Kitchen space available
- ☐ Built-in water softener
- ☐ Quick wash programme
- ☐ Quietness
- ☐ Delay timer
- ☐ Childproof locks
- ☐ Anti-flood facility
- ☐ Removable racks/baskets
- ☐ Easy-cleaning facilities
- ☐ Rinse aid and salt level indicators
- ☐ Limitations on plate sizes
- ☐ Design of door frame
- ☐ Wash temperatures available

TYPES OF DISHWASHER

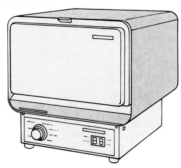

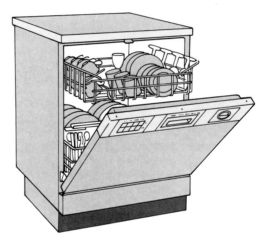

TABLE-TOP MODEL
Style Measuring approximately 47cm high, 46cm wide and 56cm deep, this model is compact enough to sit on the worksurface or a table-top and is ideal for homes where space is a problem. Although smaller in size and capacity – it takes either 4 or 6 place settings – it can cost as much to buy as a lower priced standard machine.
In use It can be plumbed in or connected to taps with a special adaptor. But enough space has to be left at the back of the machine for pipes.

FRONT-LOADING MACHINE
Style This model is the most commonplace and is approximately the same size as a standard washing machine – usually about 85cm high by 60cm wide by 60cm deep.
It has a front-opening, drop-down door which when open makes a useful place to put crockery while loading and unloading.
In use This type of dishwasher usually takes 12 international place settings, although there are one or two models around which will take 14 settings. Normally there is a range of wash programmes.
Watchpoint Some hold plates no bigger than 25.5cm diameter.

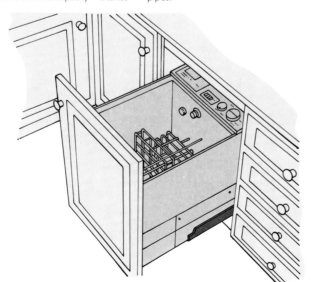

TOP-LOADING MACHINE
Style This is a recent development and is compact in size, measuring approximately 53.5cm by 40.5cm wide by 52cm deep and fits neatly into a kitchen cupboard, sliding out on rails.
In use It will take four place settings and has three programmes. Practically the same size as a compact table-top dishwasher it offers a neater solution in that it fits into a cupboard and is therefore out of sight.

INTEGRATED MODELS
Style This is a standard size machine which is specially designed to be built into a range of kitchen units. It has a choice of different decor frames into which you can insert your own panelling to match in with the rest of your kitchen units.
In use All maintenance and servicing is easily accessible from the front so that the machine does not have to be moved once it is plumbed in.

Utility Rooms

A utility room can house the washing machine and tumble dryer, cleaning equipment, ironing board, and an assortment of tools and materials for the family's various hobbies, together with a place to carry them out. Too often these activities take place in the kitchen, pushing the poor cook into a corner.

It doesn't have to be spacious – even a large cupboard or larder can be pressed into service – but a utility room does call for careful planning. If you are fitting out a small area, such as a larder or a hall cupboard, look for equipment that will stack.

A self-contained room with space for a washing machine and tumble dryer, a cupboard for cleaning materials and somewhere to keep the ironing board and iron, frees valuable space in the kitchen. An extra sink allows clothes to be soaked or flowers to be arranged without disrupting the preparation of a meal. The freezer is likely to work more efficiently in a cool utility room than in a hot kitchen. Often, too, being able to move the boiler out of a small kitchen makes planning the layout easier; sometimes even making room for an eating area.

If you can fit it in, a corner for sewing, with a wide surface to work on, and some shelves or drawers lets you leave work out without cluttering the living room. (Often getting out the machine and setting up takes as much time as the sewing.) If the sewing machine is fixed to a lift-up worktop designed for a food mixer you can house it neatly when not in use.

The site You don't need a small country manor to find space for a utility room.

The back of the garage, one side of a wide corridor, a converted rear hall or lobby can all be pressed into service. If there is room, the end of a conservatory or sun room, a rarely used dining room or even a downstairs cloakroom can be closed off with cupboard doors to conceal a utility area.

A basement or a dry cellar can be turned into a practical and useful hobbies room with all the utility equipment ranged along one wall.

Clever planning allows the utility room to double up for other uses. Kitchen units accommodate large amounts of cleaning equipment and some have special features, such as a fold-out ironing board or a trolley that rolls away neatly under a worktop.

Well fitted

The most straightforward way to plumb a room is to run all the pipework along one wall. Here kitchen units are used to house a stacked washing machine and tumble dryer. The sink has cupboards above and below and the unit at the end is tall enough to take the ironing board.

An adjustable swivel chair and an extra length of work surface opposite creates a sewing centre. Add a pinboard for hanging fabric samples, scissors and patterns.

PRACTICAL ASPECTS

Consider the hot and cold water supplies and drainage for the washing machine and sink. Think about where pipework will have to run and get an estimate for any work from a plumber before you begin. If you are fitting a washing machine in a basement you may need a pump to bring waste water up to ground level.

Efficient ventilation is another essential; rust, damp, mildew and condensation are all problems in a badly ventilated utility room. Fit an extractor fan or ventilator grid. Some are linked to the light switch, so they turn on whenever the room is used.

Tumble dryers are usually fitted with a venting kit to remove the moist, damp air. The tubing either needs to reach across to an open window or can be permanently fitted through an external wall. Some tumble dryers condense the warm air and pump the condensed water out; they need simply to have a waste pipe leading to the main drain.

Allow for plenty of electrical sockets as many of the pieces of equipment will need to remain plugged in all the time. Fit several at worktop height too, so you can run items such as an iron.

△ *Neatly styled*
There was enough room in this rear lobby for a short run of kitchen units with a washing machine and tumble dryer behind matching decor panels and a stainless steel sink with mixer tap. There is a high shelf for washing powders and a steel pole with butcher's hooks for hanging utensils neatly.

◁ *Simply concealed*
Careful choice of well-designed units maximizes storage space. A venetian blind pulls down over the 'hardwear' and the ironing board folds back into a cupboard, leaving a room that can be adapted to another use, such as a playroom or hobbies room.

Apricot coloured cupboard doors and a grey-brown tiled floor take the emphasis away from the cold white of the machines.

◁ **Corner cupboard**
There was room in this rarely used dining room to close off an alcove at one end with louvred doors, hiding a washing machine, tumble dryer and a shelf for assorted cleaning materials from view.

▽ **Stacked approach**
Alternatively, the tumble dryer can be stacked above the washing machine, freeing the space on the left.

Underneath the worktop there is room for a wire trolley with two deep drawers for sorting clothes and piling ironing. Above this is an iron tidy and a double electric socket. An eye-level, lockable cupboard keeps powders and cleaning fluids well out of children's reach.

The doors are replaced with solid wood, the left-hand one fitted with two sturdy hooks to hang a collapsible ironing board.

BRIGHT IDEA

Iron tidy Irons, especially steam irons, are best stored upright. A holder mounted on the wall lets you hang up the iron immediately after use. Made of steel, with brackets to wind the flex around, the holder can be fixed to a wall or the inside of a cupboard door.

UTILITY WATCHPOINTS

☐ Washing machines may flood occasionally, so a waterproof floor is essential. Lay ceramic or quarry tiles for long lasting good looks, or cushioned vinyl for warmth and comfort.

☐ Care should be taken to position all switches and sockets well out of the way of any water. Trailing wires should also be avoided.

☐ If machines are built under worktops, make sure that they can be pulled out for access to switches and plumbing.

☐ A track of spotlights or a fluorescent strip provides a better level of even light than a single pendant.

▷ Picture window

Brighten up a dark room or one where the window looks out on an uninspiring view with a picture blind.

This tiny utility room has a single drainer sink set into a worktop which continues over a front-loading washing machine and dryer. There is enough room to leave the ironing board standing against the other wall.

◁ Storage solutions

A place to sort dirty washing and somewhere to store clothes before ironing is a must. Newly-washed laundry should be kept well-aired. Here, plastic-coated wire drawers in a pull-out unit with slatted shelves above ensure nothing is ruined by damp.

Fit narrow shelves and cover with roller blinds if the room is too small for ordinary cupboard doors.

If there is room screw wire racks to the back of the main door, or cupboard doors, to squeeze in extra storage space. Ironing boards, brooms and mops can all be hung from a row of hooks on the wall.

▷ Shower room

A utility room plumbed for a washing machine could be the ideal place for an extra shower.

Instantaneous showers that work using incoming mains water are the ideal type to fit in a utility room as they usually need the minimum of plumbing work.

If you do have a shower in a utility room you will need to observe the same safety regulations regarding electricity as you do for a bathroom and good ventilation is essential.

Home Laundry Machines

AUTOMATIC WASHING MACHINES & WASHER-DRYERS

Your decision on the machine to buy to cope with your washing depends on two main factors. First, the size of your family and the amount of washing to be done; and second, the amount of space available in your kitchen/utility room for your home laundry equipment.

With an automatic washing machine everything is, as its name implies, automatic. You simply select the washing programme, add the detergent and fabric conditioner, put in the clothes and switch on. The machine does the rest, taking in the right amount of water, heating it to the selected temperature and dispensing first the detergent, then the conditioner.

These days you have the choice between a front-loading or a top-loading automatic machine.

Size Most models are freestanding – front-loading machines are usually a standard 85cm high, 60cm wide and 55cm deep. They can be slotted under a worktop surface or some can be built in. There are one or two smaller models available for kitchens where space is a problem, though they take a smaller load. Top-loading machines are much slimmer – around 40cm – and around the same height or slightly taller.

Capacity Front and top-loading machines take an average of 9lbs – 11lbs of dry laundry while smaller machines will only cope with about half of this amount.

Mechanism An automatic machine has a single drum container for washing, rinsing, and spin drying.

The drum – made from stainless steel or vitreous enamel – is perforated or slotted and usually has internal fins or 'lifters' which create the tumbling action in alternate directions to reduce the tangling of clothes.

Boiling also agitates water and was one of the main reasons why clothes used to be boiled. With modern detergents and machine agitation, boiling is not usually necessary.

Programmes As well as carrying out the basic operations of washing, rinsing and

spin-drying, the automatic machine also provides specific programmes to cater for a wide variety of fabrics. These can include the following:

☐ **Economy programme** For smaller wash loads this reduces the water intake, temperature and/or washing time to save power.

☐ **Biological soak or wash** Some machines offer a facility for special low-temperature washes.

☐ **Rinse and hold** Synthetic fabrics do not absorb as much water as natural ones and if they are spun too long when hot, bad creasing can occur. 'Rinse and hold' allows such fabrics to be rinsed only. This option is also useful if you want to use your machine while you're out and do not want spun-dried clothes sitting in the drum for hours after the cycle is complete.

☐ **Automatic timer** Several washing machines and washer-dryers incorporate automatic timers which allow you to pre-set the programme for day or overnight operation. (The latter can take advantage of cheaper electricity tariffs – Economy 7. In order to do this, however, you must first have an Economy 7 meter installed in your home.)

☐ **Spin speeds** Water is removed from the clothes by centrifugal force when the drum is rotated at high speed, thus the higher the spin, the faster water is extracted. Speed is measured in revolutions per minute (rpm) and varies from 400 to 1300. Some machines offer a selection of spin speeds to suit different

---

CHECKLIST

Before buying consider which features you require.
☐ Variety of programmes
☐ High spin speeds
☐ Economy features
☐ Decor panel
☐ Hot and cold water fill
☐ Childproof features
☐ Automatic timer
☐ Capacity
☐ Separate washer and dryer or a single washer/dryer unit

---

fabrics or can vary the time of spinning according to the programme selected.

Controls Machines vary but each is likely to have a single programme selector dial. Some more sophisticated models have digital push-button control with LED display instead. The most sophisticated even incorporate a special display which indicates that a fault has developed or that an incorrect programme has been selected – this is all possible thanks to the advent of the microchip!

Detergents and fabric conditioners A low lather detergent should always be used in a front-loading automatic to avoid 'over-sudsing' which results in a poor wash and can harm the machine.

Detergent dispensers usually have three compartments; one for pre-wash detergent, one for main wash detergent and one for fabric conditioner. Dispensers are filled as required before the machine is switched on and the contents automatically dispensed into the machine at the correct time during the programme. Some of the full-featured models have a conditioner tank inside the washing machine which only needs to be filled every few months – it adds conditioner automatically each time you put a wash in.

There is now an alternative to washing powder – a liquid washing detergent contained in a plastic 'ball'. Instead of filling the detergent dispenser compartment, you simply put the ball into the machine with the washing.

Siting Front-loading automatics can be fitted permanently under a worktop whereas top-loading automatics have controls along the back which must be accessible. However, the latter sometimes come supplied with a tabletop which allows you to make use of the washing machine as a work surface while not in use.

Front-loading automatic washing machines and tumble dryers can be 'stacked' one on top of the other. In order to do this, you must buy a 'stacking kit' from the manufacturer. It is best to stack machines which are made by the same manufacturer. However, there is nothing to stop you stacking different makes of machine as long as you check that the sizes are the same and you don't mind that they won't match.

Decor panels Many appliances can be bought with a decor frame which enables you to buy a dummy fascia and fit it on to the front of the machine so it matches the rest of your kitchen units.

Integrated unit Alternatively you can buy – for an extra cost – a machine which has a fascia already on it to match your kitchen units so all that can be seen is the control panel – the rest is hidden

behind the integral door.

Transit bars/brackets These are fitted to the inside of the drum to protect a machine during delivery. They must be removed before use otherwise they can cause damage. Conversely, they must be put back in place if you have to move your machine any distance.

WASHER-DRYERS

These machines, as their name implies, combine the dual functions of washing and drying in one standard-size machine. The washer-dryer looks very much like a front-loading automatic washing machine and has a single drum in which both washing and tumble drying take place.

Capacity The amount of clothes which can be washed is the same as for the front-loading automatic washing machine – between 9lb and 11lb. However, washer-dryers cannot dry an entire washing load in one go, so some of the laundry (usually about half) has to be taken out first.

Like an automatic washing machine, the washer-dryer can cope with your washing automatically once you have selected a programme.

Types There are two types of washer-dryer: those which require venting and those which are self-condensing.

The vented ones require a venting kit with hose to take away condensation, just like tumble dryers. The self-condensing versions condense steam taken from the clothes during drying back into water, which then runs out of the waste pipe. Self-condensing machines are more complex and consequently more expensive. Also they usually take about 10–15 minutes longer to complete the drying cycle and so use slightly more electricity.

TYPES OF AUTOMATIC MACHINE

FRONT-LOADING
Style Can be freestanding or built in under a work surface. Washing is loaded through the front-opening circular glass door. Controls are situated at the front.
In use Can be stacked with a tumble dryer, using a stacking kit provided by the manufacturer.

TOP-LOADING
Style These are top-opening and have controls along the back. Generally slimmer than front-loading machines – 56–61cm deep on average.
In use Easier to drop in a forgotten item when the cycle is in operation! Spin speeds are often slower than front-loading machines.

INTEGRATED
Style The appliance is adapted by its manufacturers to take a door that matches exactly those on your kitchen units.
In use All that you can see therefore is the control panel and the integral door.
Watchpoint Available at a cost!

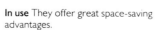

WASHER-DRYER
Style Although these machines combine the dual function of washing and drying, they are no larger than a conventional front-loading machine. They can be freestanding or built-in.

In use They offer great space-saving advantages.
Watchpoint Most washer-dryers cannot dry an entire washing load, so some of the laundry has to be taken out first.

COMPACT AUTOMATIC
Style A baby version of the front-loading automatic washing machine. It performs the same functions, but with a reduced wash load (usually about 5lbs).
In use Because of its dimensions – only 66cm high – it is ideal for single people or those living in bedsits or holiday homes.

TABLETOP AUTOMATIC
Style A lightweight and compact washing machine which requires no plumbing and simply sits on the sink draining board.
In use It fills from the hot water tap via a hose. It has an automatic programme for pre-wash, soak, five-minute final wash and three-stage rinse. Its capacity is 4½lb and it stands 47cm high, 46cm deep and 38cm wide.

TUMBLE DRYERS

When clothes or fabrics have been washed (either by hand or in a washing machine), they are usually still too wet to iron and the quickest and most reliable way to remove this excess water is to use an electric tumble dryer.

Tumble dryers use a combination of heat and mechanical movement to give quick and even drying. The wet washing is placed in a perforated steel drum through which warm air is passed. Air is drawn into the machine over heating elements and passes through the moving clothes, taking up moisture from them. The warm, moist air must be removed from the machine and there are two basic methods for doing so.

VENTING DRYERS

Here the dryer is vented to the outside through an exhaust outlet. Unless the room is particularly large and well ventilated, a venting kit will be necessary – basically, this is a pipe or tube, which is usually sold separately from the machine. The pipe is usually flexible, but can be fixed.

Flexible A large, flexible tube about 75–100mm in diameter is attached to the front, back, or side of the tumble dryer and the free end may be hung through a door or window. The tubing can be easily removed and stored when not in use.

Fixed A large diameter tube attached to the machine can be built through an outside wall as a permanent vent.

CONDENSER DRYERS

These machines are suitable for rooms where venting is not possible. In this type of machine, the moisture given off by the washing is directed on to a condenser unit, usually fitted in the base of the dryer. Here the air is cooled and the moisture condenses to water which is then removed through the waste pipe.

However, in some machines this condensed water is caught in a bottle or tank (usually in the bottom of the machine). When it is full a warning light shows on the machine and you need to empty it. The condenser dryer is generally more efficient than the vented tumble dryer.

Safety It isn't advisable to put a tumble dryer in a bathroom for safety reasons. However it is possible to get round this problem by connecting it to a fixed switched spur outside the room and enclosing it in a cupboard.

Sizes Tumble dryers are available in different sizes ranging from fairly small models which can be wall-mounted to others designed to fit beneath a standard 900mm-high worktop. To save space many models may be stacked on top of an automatic washing machine.

Capacity The amount of washing which can be dried at a time varies from model to model but ranges between 6lb and 11lb. For best results it is important not to overload the machine. It is usually better to dry two smallish loads rather than one large one, especially in the case of man-made fibres which are particularly prone to creasing.

Operation The dryer is usually operated by a minute timer which gives a range of drying times from 1–90 minutes or even 120 minutes in some models. In addition to this some machines have a heat selection switch which offers two or more heat settings.

Features Many dryers have an automatic timer which can be set to delay the start of the drying process (ie, the dryer can be set to finish at a convenient time for ironing).

Crease prevention Some machines have an anti-crease cycle which uses a cool, intermittent 'reverse tumble action' at the end of the timed programme to prevent excessive creasing.

Alternatively you can simply select the degree of dampness and a special sensor device measures the moisture content in the clothes so they come out ready to be ironed.

Advantages Tumble dryers can remove several litres of water in a relatively short space of time, but they only work really efficiently if the clothes have already been well spun. If, for example, you put clothes into the dryer which haven't first been spun, not only will they take a *very* long time to dry properly, but the electricity used is going to be far more – and certainly not cost-effective.

TYPES OF TUMBLE DRYERS

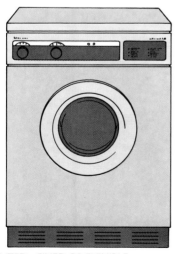

VENTED – FIXED OR FLEXIBLE

Style The moist air removed from the clothes is discharged through an air outlet which, unless the room is particularly large and well ventilated, needs to be removed through an outside wall. This can be done by a permanent fixed pipe/hose or via a flexible one which is just pushed through an open window.

In use A 'venting kit' from the manufacturer is not usually supplied with the machine so is an extra cost. Fixed venting requires making an additional permanent escape route to the outside. A dryer could be used in a cupboard.

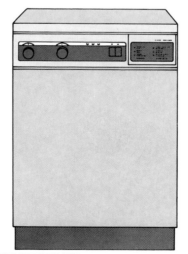

SELF-CONDENSER

Style This model condenses steam taken from the washing during drying back into water, which is either stored in an integral removable container or simply runs out through the waste-pipe.

In use Easy to install since no venting is necessary. (A vented dryer has to be sited near a window so the hose can be put out of it, but with the condenser there are no restrictions about positioning.) More efficient than vented machines, condenser dryers tend to be more expensive to buy and to run.

CHECKLIST

Before making your final choice of tumble dryer consider the availability of the following and their importance to you:
☐ Capacity
☐ Sensor control
☐ Delay timer
☐ Condenser or vented tumble dryer
☐ Reverse tumble action
☐ Range of drying times
☐ Colour of appliance
☐ Will it stack on top of your washing machine?

If you want the two machines to stack neatly, you will do best to buy a dryer which is the same make as your automatic.

SINGLE TUB AND TWIN TUB WASHING MACHINES

Single-tub washing machines have a washing container only, as the name suggests. Twin-tub machines have a washer and spin dryer assembled side by side in an outer casing.

Construction Single and twin-tub washing machines have round or square tubs and are usually constructed in stainless steel or vitreous-enamelled steel. They are filled with water via a hose which you have to connect to the end of your tap. A 2–3kW heater under or on the base of the tub heats the water to the required washing temperature. Then the tub is ready to wash. (The heater has an automatic cut-out which operates when there is no water in the tub.)

Capacity Most take up to 3.2kg of dry laundry and 30–43 litres of water. The machines always have castors so they can be wheeled from where they are kept to a position nearer the sink.

Washing action There are two main types of washing action: a central spindle agitator, or an impeller or rotating wheel, positioned at the side or bottom of the tub. Detergent is dissolved in the water before clothes are added.

Controls The twin-tub washing machine can be divided broadly into three types according to their degree of control:

☐ The user switches on the heater, then switches it off when the water is hot enough. The minute timer is then set and the motor switched on, so that washing can begin. The motor will then switch itself off when the washing time which is set on the minute timer is finished.

☐ The heater control is set to the desired temperature and when the water reaches this, the heater switches itself off. The minute timer is then set and the motor is switched on so that washing begins. As with the first type, the motor switches itself off when the washing time set on the minute timer is finished.

Temperature and timer controls are linked and switch the machine on to wash as soon as the required temperature is reached. After the correct time, the machine switches off.

Rinsing and drying After washing items in a single-tub or twin-tub machine, they can be transferred to a spin dryer. To rinse in a spin dryer, water is introduced by a hose or jet from the tap and then spun away in the sink. The spin dryer removes water from the clothes by centrifugal force. The drum is rotated at high speed by an electric motor, clothes are forced against the sides of the container and water drains off through slots or holes. The water is then piped away via a hose to the sink.

Water extraction The amount of water removed depends upon the spin speed and diameter of the container. Models vary in speed from 1300–3000 rpm.

Safety Spin dryers all have lid safety devices which prevent access to the container during spinning. The lid cannot be opened until spinning has completely stopped.

Advantages Water from the spin dryer can be pumped back into the wash tub and used again. Another advantage is that you can wash a second load in the washing machine while rinsing and spinning the first. The tub can be used to boil, bleach, or dye clothes.

Disadvantages These machines have a smaller capacity than automatics and cannot be left completely unattended.

TYPES OF SINGLE/TWIN-TUB MACHINES

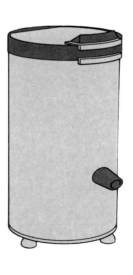

SINGLE TUB
Style This model has a round or square tub with a top opening. Slimmer in width than the standard front loader, but it fits under a worksurface.
In use It is not automatic and requires supervision. Certain manufacturers provide a single-tub washing machine and a separate spin dryer that can be linked with a bridge attachment. This arrangement is ideal where space is limited since the machines can be positioned side by side or separately.

SPIN DRYER
Style A copper-clad spin dryer designed to be used with a single-tub washing machine or when you have washed clothes by hand.
In use This stands at just below work surface height so it can be tucked under a countertop. Instead of a hose which has to be put into a sink so the water extracted from washing can go out through the waste, this machine has a gravity drain spout. You simply put a bucket or bowl below the spout to catch the extracted water. Available in two sizes: 5lb or 7½lb spinning capacity.

TWIN TUB
Style This combines the washing and spinning in the same machine. It fits under the work surface. Its lid is a laminated wood-effect worktop.
In use It is not plumbed in and has to be filled by a hose from the tap. (Water from the spin dryer also comes out via a hose into kitchen sink.)
Watchpoint Those on castors can be moved easily – bearing in mind that most people have to move them to get them near to the sink.

INDEX

PHOTOGRAPHIC CREDITS
1 Woodstock, 2-3 Leicht Kitchens, 4-5 Hygena, 6 EWA/Rodney Hyett, 13 Schreiber Furniture Ltd, 14 & 15 Jalag/Zuhause, 16 Winchmore, 17(t) Bulthaup, 17(b) Qualcast (Fleetway) Ltd, 18(tl) EWA/Michael Dunne, 18(tr) Jalag/Zuhause, 18(b) Wrighton International, 19 National Magazine Co/David Brittain, 20 EWA/Spike Powell, 21 PWA/Living Magazine, 22 Smallbone of Devizes, 23 EWA/Rodney Hyett, 24(t) PWA/International, 24(b) Bosch, 25 Jalag/Zuhause, 26-7 Poggenpohl, 28 EWA/Tom Leighton, 29(t) Poggenpohl, 29(b) Cover Plus from Woolworth, 30(t) Stelrad Group, 30(b) EWA/Spike Powell, 31 Miele, 32 Smallbone of Devizes, 33 B & Q DIY Supercentres, 34(t) Habitat, 34(b) Woodstock, 35 Jerry Tubby/Eaglemoss, 36 EWA/ Michael Nicholson, 37(t) Arcaid/Richard Bryant, 37(b) C.P. Hart/Aqua Ware, 38 Be Modern, 39(t) Bosch, 39(bl) SieMatic, 39(br) Jalag/Zuhause, 40(t) Vymura International, 40(bl) Martyn Goddard, 40(br) EWA/Rodney Hyett, 41 National Magazine Co/Good Housekeeping, 42 Leicht Furniture Ltd, 43(t) EWA/Michael Nicholson, 43(b) Jalag/Zuhause, 44-5 Bulthaup, 45(tr) Poggenpohl, 45(bl) EWA/ Rodney Hyett, 45(br) Bulthaup, 46 EWA/ Rodney Hyett, 47 EWA/Jerry Tubby, 48-9 EWA/Michael Dunne, 50(t) The Original Kitchen Co, 50(b) C.P. Hart/Aqua Ware, 51 EWA/Clive Helm, 52(t) EWA/Michael Dunne, 52(b) EWA/Neil Lorimer, 53 EWA/ Spike Powell, 54(t) Cristal Tiles, 54(b) Formica Ltd, 55 PWA/International, 56(t) Jalag/ Zuhause, 56(b) Woodstock, 57(t) EWA/Clive Helm, 57(b)SieMatic, 58(tl) Moben Kitchens, 58(tr) Woodstock, 58(b) Syndication International/Homes and Gardens, 59 & 60-1 National Magazine Co/Jan Baldwin, 60(b) Schreiber Furniture Ltd, 61(t) Smallbone of Devizes, 61(b) Richard Paul, 62 EWA, 63(t) EWA/Rodney Hyett, 63(b) Magnet, 64(t) The Picture Library, 64(b) EWA/Michael Dunne, 65(t) EWA/Jerry Tubby, 65(b) Bosch, 66(tl) Be Modern, 66(tr) Bosch, 66(b) EWA, 87 Miele, 88(t) Bulthaup, 88(b) EWA/Rodney Hyett, 89 Dulux, 90(t) EWA/Spike Powell, 90(m) Elfa Systems, 90(b) PWA/International. Front cover: (tl) Churchill kitchen by B&Q; (tr) Robert Harding Syndication/IPC Magazines/Dominic Blackmore; (bl) Montana kitchen by Magnet; (br) Shaker kitchen by Magnet.
(EWA - Elizabeth Whiting and Associates)

'Chris Mitchell has authenticity in terms of knowing Asperger's Syndrome from a personal perspective and from having himself experienced the benefits of mindfulness. Incorporating mindfulness in everyday life will have a positive effect on all the core characteristics of Asperger's Syndrome. Reading this book has the potential to be a life-changing experience for those who have Asperger's Syndrome.'

— *Tony Attwood, Clinical Psychologist, Minds & Hearts Clinic, Australia, and author of* The Complete Guide to Asperger's Syndrome

'I have known Chris for a number of years and this book reflects his calm, insightful attitude towards life and Asperger Syndrome's very well indeed. There are some wonderful intuitions, even philosophies, in this book that will be beneficial for many people associated with Asperger's Syndrome.'

— *Dr Luke Beardon, Senior Lecturer in Autism at The Autism Centre, Sheffield Hallam University, UK*

'This book opens with a very supportive introduction for both the person with Asperger's Syndrome considering mindfulness and the professional who may be supporting them. Chris writes in a clear and expressive manner showing a true understanding of both Asperger's Syndrome and mindfulness. I really feel like I have shared in part of Chris's journey and gained along the way.'

— *Janet Ashfield, life coach and mindfulness practitioner*

'As an autistic person who knows the value of mindfulness, I would recommend this book to anyone wanting to gain greater awareness of themselves and live more peacefully. Using great analogies, Chris shows how we can manage the stresses of an autism spectrum condition using simple exercises to deal with little things that can build into debilitating stress and ill health.'

— *Zaffy Simone, autistic adult, independent autism consultant and illustrator*

by the same author

Asperger's Syndrome and Mindfulness
Taking Refuge in the Buddha
ISBN 978 1 84310 686 9
eISBN 978 1 84642 888 3

of related interest

Meditation for Aspies
Everyday Techniques to Help People with Asperger Syndrome
Take Control and Improve their Lives
Ulrike Domenika Bolls
ISBN 978 1 84905 386 0
eISBN 978 0 85700 756 8

Mind/Body Techniques for Asperger's Syndrome
The Way of the Pathfinder
Ron Rubio
Forewords by Irene Brody and Anthony Castrogiovanni
ISBN 978 1 84310 875 7
eISBN 978 1 84642 805 0

The Complete Guide to Asperger's Syndrome
Tony Attwood
ISBN 978 1 84310 495 7 (hardback)
ISBN 978 1 84310 669 2 (paperback)
eISBN 978 1 84642 559 2

Asperger Syndrome and Anxiety
A Guide to Successful Stress Management
Nick Dubin
Foreword by Valerie Gaus
ISBN 978 1 84310 895 5
eISBN 978 1 84642 922 4

A Self-Determined Future with Asperger Syndrome
Solution Focused Approaches
E. Veronica Bliss and Genevieve Edmonds
ISBN 978 1 84310 513 8
eISBN 978 1 84642 685 8